ALL OF ME

Patsy Palmer

BBC

LARGE PRINT

First published 2007
by
Hodder & Stoughton
This Large Print edition published 2008
by
BBC Audiobooks Ltd
by arrangement with
Hodder & Stoughton

UK Hardcover ISBN 978 1 405 64875 2
UK Softcover   ISBN 978 1 405 64876 9

British Library Cataloguing in Publication Data available

Printed and bound in Great Britain by
CPI Antony Rowe, Eastbourne

I dedicate this book to Charley, Fenton and Emilia
... Love is all you need. Never, ever believe the lie!

> If I had to do it all again
> I wouldn't take away the rain
> Cuz I know it made me who I am
>   Faith Evans, 'Again'

ACKNOWLEDGEMENTS

I would like to express my sincere thanks to everyone I have been privileged to share moments of my journey with, and to those who are still in my life and, please God, will remain so.

In no particular order: Caro Handley, who helped me structure this book, who has the patience of a saint and who allowed me to see my words on paper. The editorial staff at Hodder, especially Rowena Webb and Helen Coyle, who have been both kind and wise. Paul Stevens and Kate Buckley, who have given me such guidance along my career path.

Charlotte Cutler my faithful friend and business partner whom I love dearly and who looks great with a tan! Etta, Daniel, Fran and Mercy for blessing my life with her sister. My girlies, George, Brooke, Jo, Lily, Lisa, Alex, Finn, Kerry, Selina, Pru, Simone—weren't there some long nights! Thanks for the laughs Dark Angels!! Nicole my gorgeous oldest friend, thanks udder! Anna Scher, what a wonderful teacher who gives kids like us a chance to shine their light. Louise, Danny, Katie, Archie, Scarlett, Dolcie, for helping me see the truth and being in Brighton to help us. Mary, Nicky, Pat, Annabel, Dave the builder, and Sarah. Hazeem El Rafeay, for saving our lives! Neil for the hotel room, Carluccios for the malanos and food to help me write, Tom Alsworth for all your faith in Palmer-Cutler, the Gavins for the year's blow-dries!

To all my family, those I don't see much and

those I do: Tessa, Darren, Vanessa, Amy, Sam, Zac, Jac, Arty. Jackie for being a human cookbook, and a wonderful Nan and mother-in-law. Harry for being a kind patient and loving brother and Lyndsey, Molly and Grace. Albert, just keep the faith. Dad and Marcelle for always being there and never in judgement. Mum for never letting me down, for protecting me, for making sure I never ever wanted for anything and for showing me how to work hard and live well. Ted for being the most generous man I have ever met, for coming into our mad family and staying, for teaching me common sense and loving me and my mum.

Richie, the love of my life, my beautiful husband and father to our three children, you have given me love I could only ever have dreamed of! (And you can be quite funny sometimes too). My *wonderful* children: Charley, I love you, you have made my life worth living (even if the hair wax has cost a fortune, gypsy boy); Fenton, I love you, you are very special (keep dancing, may the force always be with you); Emilia, I love you, you are the most beautiful girl in the world (keep laughing, cheeky), Missi loves you.

For those who are in heaven: Norah, Farvey, Granny, Grandad, Mel, Jason, Jarrod, Darren, Danny, Mark, Stephen B, Layla, Bod, Kate. Miss you.

If I've missed anyone out, I am grateful for your contribution along the way. You know who you are. Thank you, thank you, thank you!!

Love, Julie xxx

CONTENTS

INTRODUCTION

A September day, the sun shining. An ordinary day. I'd washed and dressed, got the children out of bed, fed them and dropped them off at school, then had a quick chat on the phone with my husband, who was at work driving his cab. It was nine-fifteen and I was on my own. I had a very important appointment at one o'clock. Had to be sure to make that. But it was hours away. And in the meantime I was battling with myself: the same battle I fought—and lost—every day.

On this particular morning I was more determined than ever. I wasn't going to give in. *Not today*, I told myself. But already I felt clammy, powerless and obsessed. My hands were shaking as I looked at the Rizla papers on the side. The night before, I'd put away the puff—my skunk weed, otherwise known as super-strong marijuana—on top of a cupboard, hoping that when I woke up in the morning I'd have forgotten about it. That was almost funny. I must have been mad to imagine I could forget it—I couldn't think about anything else.

I opened the back door to get some air. Lately I'd begun to experience this terrible feeling all the time that someone was behind me. A part of me knew I was getting paranoid and that it was caused by the drugs—but most of the time I didn't listen to that part of me and just kept looking over my shoulder. The feeling made me edgy. Maybe the fresh air would help.

It didn't. *Do something normal*, I told myself. So

I took the vacuum cleaner out of the cupboard. I loathe housework, but it was the most normal thing I could think of. I still had plenty of time before my very important appointment. And surely I would feel better as soon as I'd done the vacuuming.

As I started pushing the machine around I felt agitated. All I wanted was to reach on top of the cupboard and begin the ritual again. *It'll be different today*, I thought. *I won't have much—just a little puff to calm me down, stop me feeling so tense.* That wouldn't matter, would it—just a puff or two? . . . But what about my really, really important appointment at one o'clock? *Oh, just cancel it*, said the voice in my head. *Make up an excuse. They won't know.*

So I picked up the phone and cancelled the meeting. Then I made sure I had enough food in the fridge for my favourite Halloumi delight— Halloumi cheese, bacon, pitta bread, juicy beef tomatoes—because skunk weed always made me very hungry. All ready. Shut fridge, grab Rizlas, fags and weed. Roll.

A minute later I was on the couch, watching *This Morning* and smoking a big fat joint. I'd promised myself never to smoke in the house because of the kids. Didn't want any traces lingering for them. Wanted to be extra-careful because my little girl had chest problems. And I was a responsible parent—of course I was. So I'd only have a little— half a joint—then open the windows and clear the air. Save the other half for later, after the kids were in bed.

After a few puffs I got the relief I craved. All the sweating, the agitation and the tension in my body dissolved. Everything seemed to be under control again. It wasn't, of course, and deep down I knew it. But denial is more powerful than anything, even skunk weed.

After I'd eaten my Halloumi delight the buzz began to wear off. The guilt was kicking in, but it was all right because I was going to do the ironing and that was something normal and responsible. I could still be the lovely mum I wanted to be. Only I was desperate for another little high. Maybe it would be OK to smoke the other half of the joint. Plenty of time to clear the air and iron. After all, it was still only eleven o'clock.

By midday I was completely stoned. But that was OK, because I could eat something more and be fine by three-thirty, when I needed to leave on the school run.

Three hours later I had finished my third joint and second jam doughnut. I stood in the middle of the room and thought, *Is this what my life has come to?* It wasn't very dramatic as revelations go. I wasn't suicidal, I wasn't homeless, I had money, I still had a career, I still had a marriage and my kids. But that day I knew I was beaten emotionally, unable even to cry for the years of self-abuse I'd gone through. And I understood, for the first time, that I was an addict.

The pattern of that day had been repeated for years. But until then I had never really wanted to stop smoking. Not enough. I didn't think it was so bad—after all the hard drugs and alcohol that I'd used over the years—to get a little bit stoned each day. Or so I told myself. I'd had help with all the other stuff. Been to clinics, meetings, the lot. I suppose it did help at the time—but never for long. I'd always start again, sometimes with a different drug or another type of drink, but it was the same old pattern. And I'd tell myself every time that it was OK because I could manage it, I wasn't addicted any more, I wasn't taking the really hard stuff—I'd never taken heroin, for goodness' sake! I could enjoy myself, I reckoned, and keep things under control.

It's called believing the lie, and it's a place I'd known since I was eight years old and I first started secretly downing the dregs in the glasses at adult parties. I began smoking marijuana at eleven, and by the time I was in my twenties I was bingeing my life away on cocaine, Ecstasy and vodka. I would be out of my head for two or three days in a row, and took so many drugs that I'm amazed I survived. I'd be violently sick, then I'd go back and take more until I was sick again. My finger was always hovering over that self-destruct button.

Taking drugs is a bit like having a brand-new car full of petrol. At first you're so excited you can't believe how good it feels, just cruising along in your wonderful car. But gradually the petrol runs low and the engine starts nagging, so you pull over, turn the engine off and take a breather. You refuel, the engine is restored and once again you fly down that road excited and happy, leaving the past behind and forgetting there was ever a problem. Only on each occasion you do this the high lasts a shorter time, and soon a new feeling emerges, a feeling that something is wrong. The answer, you're convinced, is more petrol. You fill up, but now the petrol lasts no time at all and eventually the engine begins to fail even when the tank is full. No amount of fuel will ever get the car performing the way it once did, but you can't see that. So you start sticking obscene quantities of all kinds of other things into the tank in an attempt to get the vehicle going again and re-create the wonderful buzz you had.

Refusal to admit what's happening can keep you doing this for years. It's like wearing a pair of shades—a shiny new brand called Liars—which stop you seeing anything clearly. Those Liars are so attractive, and when you're wearing them you can keep on kidding yourself that if you only find the right fuel, or combination of fuels, your car will be as good as new again. As long as you keep wearing your shades you can lie, cheat, steal, hurt other people, damage yourself, go insane or even die trying to get that car back the way it was. That September day, standing in the living room wondering what I had come to, I finally took off those shades.

I left the house to go to my kids' school, still stoned, and went through the same paranoid routine I'd followed every day for months. I'd wait outside, hiding behind my turned up collar, wanting to die, avoiding all the other parents and talking to no one. The voice in my head would be saying, *What a fucking nightmare this is! I'm trapped, can't move, can't open my mouth to speak. OK, focus on the dustbin down to your right, then you won't have to look at anyone.* I didn't know any of the other mums or dads—my behaviour must have seemed so aloof that they were scared to approach me. They've told me since that the signals I gave out said, *Keep away from me.* The few who ventured a smile in my direction got the top of my head in response, as I got out my phone and huddled over it, pretending to make calls. I cringe

5

when I recall this now because it wasn't how I wanted to be at all, but I was quite unable to function normally. I longed to join in with their laughter and chat about going home for tea and after-school clubs. But between me, in my isolation, and them was a vast gulf which I had no idea how to cross. I've since become good friends with many of the parents, and apologized for my behaviour, but to get to that point I had to take a huge step forward, out of denial, in order to face the truth.

When I got home that afternoon I knew it was over. I don't know why that day was different— after all, I'd tried to stop a good many times before and I'd been in many painful, humiliating and horrible situations that hadn't been enough to stop me. But somehow that day I knew I'd reached the end of a long road. Twenty-four years after my first drink, almost as long since my first taste of drugs, I was ready to quit.

I wanted to live again, to wake up and feel part of life, to hug my kids, play with them, be with my husband, work, walk down the street, turn up for appointments, make friends—and to do so without hiding behind the haze that goes with drugs. I wanted to feel, think and see clearly. All my life I'd felt I was on the outside looking in, never quite part of anything, a little bit scared. Drugs and drink had taken away that feeling and had given me the courage to be loud and aggressive, but they hadn't given me the one thing I really wanted—to belong. I was going to have to find that on my own.

Luckily I knew where to go for help. The next day I walked into a convention of hundreds of addicts and alcoholics just like me. It wasn't the first time—I'd been going to meetings of this sort

6

on and off for nine years. But every time I'd slipped back to the drink and drugs. One of my closest friends was there. I hadn't seen her for a while, so I sat next to her and she smiled, glad to see me. She'd been happy without the drugs or booze for a good while, and I wanted to be in the same place with her.

There was a lot said at that convention that I'd never heard—or perhaps never really taken in—before. Until then I'd thought that places and people were responsible for the way I'd turned out, and had no idea that I might be responsible myself. I didn't understand real responsibility. By that I don't mean earning a living—I'd been doing that since I was six years old and first stepped on to a stage—or paying bills or running a house or even being a parent. I mean real grown up emotional responsibility. What on earth was that?

Since that day I've learned just what it is. Emotional responsibility gives us freedom, it gives us the strength to walk away from self-abuse, and it takes us back to who we really are. From the age of eight I'd been Patsy Palmer, actress and celebrity. Now the time had come to rediscover the real me.

1

THE BABY

I was born on 26 May 1972 in Bethnal Green Hospital in London's East End. Mum always said I was the longest baby in the hospital, though no one can remember exactly how long I was. I've heard the story of the midwife who delivered me so many times I used to think I knew her. My mother said she'd never forget her—she was so small that Mum could only see the top of her Afro hairdo as she giggled loudly and hysterically all through labour, while Mum, with a shriek and an almighty push, brought me into the world.

I was named Julie Anne—Julie after a friend of my mum's and Anne after Mum herself, who was called Patricia Ann (and known as Pat). Mum said Julie was beautiful as well as being a lovely person, and she hoped I'd grow up to be the same. Everyone was glad I was a girl because my parents already had two sons, Harry and Albert, aged eight and five. After two boys Mum couldn't quite believe she had a girl and for the first day just stared at me in disbelief. The other surprise was my bright red hair. Harry was white-blond, Albert jet-black, so a redhead was the last thing my parents expected. Red hair didn't exactly run in the family, but my great-grandfather had been known as Ginger and so, although it had skipped a couple of generations, I can't have been the first.

The day after I was born Mum's doting eyes left my face for a split second and there it was, the creature that got her out of bed so fast she was home that very day, much to the disapproval of the nurses. Mum had a phobia about creepy-crawlies, especially dirty great cockroaches like the one on the hospital floor. She was told by the nurse, with a wagging finger, 'If you go home now, Mrs Harris, you'll have no midwife to look after you—you're supposed to stay here for ten days.' As Mum clambered into her clothes, with me under one arm, the nurse added, 'What are you so upset about? There are hundreds of cockroaches in this hospital.'

'Well, there are none in my flat!' my mother shouted, and marched out of the door to where my dad was waiting to drive us home in the back of his taxi.

Home for the Harris family was a second-floor, three-bedroom council flat in a red-brick block, just round the corner from the Columbia Road flower market. It couldn't have been more of a contrast to the filthy hospital—spanking clean thanks to my grandmother Norah, Mum's mother, who had been scrubbing and polishing for hours in anticipation of our return. My first memories are of that flat, which had a large kitchen where we'd all eat together, and a living room with French windows. There was no balcony outside them, just iron railings—but the view from those windows ran the whole length of Old Bethnal Green Road.

My mother was twenty-eight when she had me, which was getting on a bit even for your third child in those days. She only looked about fourteen, though. She had brown hair with a hint of auburn, hazel eyes and a lovely curvaceous figure—she wore polo-necks and mini-skirts and looked like

Jaclyn Smith, original seventies' star of *Charlie's Angels*. Mum was a strong woman who, no doubt partly as a result of a tough childhood, kept her vulnerability locked deep inside. Her kids came first: she was determined to give us a good start and was always there for us with hugs and advice. She often told me that I was beautiful, and I adored her. She wasn't a pushover, though—she only had to give me what I called 'the look' and I'd stop misbehaving and instantly do as I was told, knowing that otherwise I'd be in big trouble. And if any of us kids pushed her too far we'd get a quick wallop.

My dad, Albert, was a quieter and more distant figure in our lives. A good-looking man with black hair, he worked long hours driving his cab, and when he got home he soon headed out again to the pub. As a kid, when I was around him we didn't really connect. I knew he cared, but he didn't often show affection and I don't remember us ever really talking. The times we spent together were Sunday afternoons, when he used to take me to the pub with him to give Mum a bit of space—he drank gin and tonic and I liked the smell of it. The other place he used to take me for a treat sometimes was the green huts down on the Embankment, where the cabbies had their breakfast.

From the start I was the baby of the family, the much-loved little girl who'd come along when the other babies were well on the way to growing up. My parents, grandparents, aunts, uncles, cousins and big brothers all fussed over me, played with me and looked after me. Until I was three and went to nursery, Mum was at home and I was almost always with her. She used to wheel me around Columbia

11

Road in my pram, shopping, meeting friends and showing me off. She says I talked long before I could walk, and that doesn't surprise anyone who knows me. Apparently by the age of nine months I would say 'Hello'—or my version of it—to everyone, and startled shoppers used to look into my pram and exclaim, 'That baby just spoke!' Mum would smile and say, 'Yes, she did', and I'd be babbling away again. When she took me with her to collect my brother Albert from school I'd be in the playground shouting his name out from my pram.

By the age of one I was walking, and by fifteen months I was singing little songs and dancing. I loved putting on a show for my parents' friends when they came round. But, proud as they were, my parents didn't think for a second that I might really grow up to be a performer. After all, there was no history of it on either side of the family— the men mostly drove cabs and the women worked in the East End's many clothing factories. There were so many cab drivers in our family that when I was small I thought all men drove cabs.

At sixteen, after a few months as a typist, which she hated, Mum joined the factory where most of her friends worked. She became a machinist, making coats and suits, and by the time her children came along she had become a brilliant dressmaker who was able to make most of our clothes. Before this happened, at nineteen Mum went to work for a man called Martin Stockman. He was a fantastic boss, funny, kind and good to his workers, and she worked for him on and off for the next twenty years. While she was having children she took time off, but Martin would let her go in and work whenever she needed a bit of extra money, taking us with her.

The factory always smelled of steam from the big pressing machine—that smell, and the sound of laughter, were what hit me every time I went in. I remember all Mum's friends there, a bunch of warm, generous-spirited women who helped sort each other's problems out. There was always some drama going on with someone's husband, boyfriend or kids, but no matter how bad the situation there was always humour. It was Martin who liked to claim he'd given me my first wage packet. He would let me sit on the floor cutting the cotton fabrics. All the women got paid in little brown envelopes, and he'd put a few pennies in an envelope and give them to me. He was a lovely man, and Mum stayed friends with him until he died in the early 2000s.

As a small girl, when I wasn't with my mum I was with my nan—they were the central figures in my life. That was how it was in the East End: if mothers worked, grandmothers took over. My grandparents, especially my mum's parents, were important to us. Norah and Harry Palmer, whom we called Nor and Farvy and whose surname I would later adopt for stage purposes, lived round the corner and we saw them every day. Their one-bedroom flat was in Temple Street, on the third floor, up what seemed to me to be endless stairs. I remember how old-fashioned the place was—their beds were covered with candlewick bedspreads in pink and pale blue, and the loo had black and white tiles on the floor and a really heavy chain I could barely manage to pull.

Nor was always cleaning—her flat and ours. She was obsessive about dirt and no speck of dust was allowed to settle as she bustled about, cloths in one hand, polish in the other. When she wasn't cleaning she was sitting in her small kitchen smoking. I loved Nor dearly, and in return she doted on me and was always ready with a cuddle when I climbed on to her knee. She'd sit beside me on the sofa and tickle my back—for which I loved—for hours with her long nails while we watched old black-and-white films and I dreamed I was Shirley Temple.

She was a lovely-looking woman, slim and elegant with green eyes and long auburn hair down to her bum. She was also tiny—under five feet tall, with the most glamorous size two shoes in Bethnal Green—and even at fifty-eight she could still do the splits and handstands up the wall, which she would do to entertain me. But her beautiful face was often sad, and now that she's gone it's hard to find a photo of her in which she's smiling—more often she looks angry or distant. Her life was harder and much more complicated than I, as a small child, could have known. Only later was I told that her cleaning compulsion was actually a disorder and that she had also been diagnosed with mild schizophrenia. Nor would regularly take off, sometimes for days on end—often without telling anyone where she was going. Occasionally she took me with her, which I regarded as an adventure. We'd get on a bus and travel for hours until eventually she brought me home, none the wiser. Sometimes we'd go to Dalston and then get the bus all the way to Southend, which to me was a million miles from Bethnal Green, so it felt like a big day out. And then Nor had an old neighbour, known as Aunt Doll, who'd moved to Brighton and on occasion we'd go to see her. Every woman in the

14

East End was your 'auntie' in those days, and although it got confusing at times it did symbolize our strong sense of community. Doll had a granddaughter called Paris with curly ginger hair, which made us look as though we were real cousins—and we both liked to pretend we were.

I thought our outings were a big treat. But the reality for Norah was that she was probably desperate to escape from home for a while, because life with Farvy was far from easy. He was a big man, handsome and broad, with enormous hands, a big smile and a loud voice. He always wore a shirt and trousers, with braces. A cab driver, like his father before him, he was very sociable. While pictures of Nor at get-togethers show her sitting rigid as a statue, Farvy usually has his arm thrown possessively around her, a broad smile on his florid face, clearly a little the worse for wear. Farvy really was larger than life: he survived a brain tumour and lung cancer and came back fighting. When I asked him later how he'd done it, he waved his arm and said, 'I fucked it all off!' With Farvy, every other word was a swearword. He was brash and loud, and I idolized him.

Farvy also had a very dark side, but as a small child I never knew about it. The grandfather I knew was funny and cuddly, a gifted pianist who only had to hear a piece of music once to be able to play it. He couldn't read a note, but the two of us sat for hours taping songs off the wireless, making long lists of who they were by and then singing them into the microphone. We loved Dinah Washington, Ella Fitzgerald, big band music and Frank Sinatra. He taught me to play tunes on the piano, and used to boast that at the age of two I could play 'London's Burning'.

As I got older, however, I began to see the other aspects of Farvy—he was a terrible racist, for instance, and I felt embarrassed when I heard him sounding off about it. I remember when he was in hospital he insulted all the black nurses—but happily they just laughed at him and teased him back. They seemed to be fond of my grandfather, despite his appalling comments. Nor had I any idea until I was much older that Farvy was a gambler, even though as a little girl I used to go up the road for him to get his bread and milk and put his bet on at the bookie's. I always forgot whether it was 'each way' or 'to win', so Farvy would write it out and the man in the bookie's would do it for me. I had no idea at that age what betting was all about, but I'd remember us watching the races on TV and shouting the winners on. He liked me to shout their names, too, which he said brought good luck. I thought it was just a game, and didn't understand that week after week that was where his money was going.

Neither did I know that he used to beat his wife, tiny Norah. Mum was their only child, and she had a tough time. As a small girl she used to find her mother cowering in a corner, covered in blood, after a beating from Farvy. Mum used to say to her, 'Don't speak', because she thought that if Nor said nothing, Farvy wouldn't hit her. Later she felt guilty for thinking that her mother provoked the beatings, or could somehow have prevented them by keeping quiet. Nor suffered this physical abuse with quiet dignity and never left her husband, nursing him through all his ill health and putting up with his gambling. Why she stayed I don't know—perhaps it

16

was simply what women of her generation did.

When, after they had both died, I learned the truth about what Farvy did to Nor, I found it very difficult to come to terms with. I had worshipped Farvy, but I only ever saw a part of him. Discovering that he could be a monster was painful.

The situation at home took its toll on my future mum, and by the time she was in her late teens she was bulimic. Day after day she would eat and then throw up. She got over this problem, but she was never a big eater. I remember her cooking tea for us—egg and chips or pie and mash—and standing near the table while the rest of us ate, saying, 'I'll just have a little bit' or 'I'll have something later.' I didn't think about it at the time—it was just how things were.

Mum had met Dad in a pub when she was seventeen and he was twenty-five. He was a friend of her cousin's, and from the moment they met they were together. Although eight years younger, Mum appeared to be the stronger personality: she was outgoing and talkative, while Dad was much quieter and more introverted. A year later, in 1962, they married in Shoreditch Town Hall with their parents, Dad's sisters and a small handful of friends in attendance. Afterwards they went back to Dad's parents' flat for a roast beef dinner, and then the new Mr and Mrs Harris travelled to Jersey where they had a week's honeymoon in a boarding house by the sea.

Their first home was with Norah and Farvy, who at that time lived in north London. But soon Mum and Dad moved into a small rented flat in a house in Bethnal Green and then into the larger one

17

where they were living when I was born. Dad drove a minicab at first, then went with Farvy to work in Bishopsgate unloading goods trains. It was a few years later that Dad did the Knowledge—the incredibly tough test that all London black-cab drivers have to pass—and got his first cab. Then Farvy decided he wanted to be a cab driver too, despite the fact that he was in his late forties and didn't even have a driving licence. But he studied for the Knowledge while learning to drive, and passed both tests one after the other.

My brother Harry came along a year after my parents married, and Albert was born just over two years later. Dad's parents were Irish Catholics, and we three children were baptized in that religion. As a small girl I used to go with May, his mother, whom we called Granny, to the local Catholic church, while Nor would take me to the equivalent Church of England one. I was quite happy whichever I went to, and was tickled to learn later that Norah also had Jewish blood.

May's husband Albert had died before I was born and her life revolved around her children: Dad and his three sisters, Amelia, Helen and Jackie. All of us, typically of the East End, lived close to each other. Another brother, Fergus, had died as a baby—an enduring sadness for Granny, who often talked of him. I loved all three of my aunties, who threw big family parties at which everyone would drink too much and then sing. We all loved music, and I can remember being upstairs with my cousins and hearing the adults downstairs roaring out Neil Diamond and Barry Manilow songs.

Auntie Amelia was a mother earth figure—her

18

husband Melvin was Jewish and they had three boys and two girls. They were a warm, very close family and I loved being with them. When I got a little older I often stayed over at Auntie Amelia's and she made up a bed for me on their sofa. I usually ended up crying for my mum in the middle of the night, but by the morning I'd forgotten all about it and wanted to stay again. I used to like being at Auntie Helen's house, too. She was married to Jerry, a builder, and they lived in a flat in Poplar with their son and two daughters. One of the girls, another Amelia, was the same age as me, and so was Auntie Amelia's son Fenton, so the three of us played together a lot. We could play out safely even when we were very small because Auntie Helen could see us from her windows. There were lots of other kids in the neighbouring flats and we all played together—I had a great time there and never wanted to go home. It wasn't that home was an unhappy place, far from it but it was often just me and Mum and I always wanted to be surrounded by company—family or friends. In fact I craved the security I found in other people.

Despite my love of singing and dancing I was a timid, shy child, afraid of all kinds of things. I used to creep into Mum's side of my parents' bed most nights for comfort. I was frightened of so much—loud strangers, roads, cars, trains, in fact anything that seemed overwhelming or out of control. It never took much to start me crying, and Mum used to worry that I was too fearful.

There was one incident which might have been frightening for any child, but which sent me into an absolute paroxysm of terror. We were out shopping one day when Mum got into a fight with another woman. A feud had been building up, and when they met in the street they started rowing. Within minutes they were shouting, tussling and pulling each other's hair. I sat in my pushchair sobbing hysterically and, though the fight was soon over, it was a long time before I calmed down. That incident, I hasten to add, wasn't typical of Mum at all. Although she was direct and spoke her mind, that was the only time she ever got into a physical fight.

Mum probably hoped that I'd come out of my shell somewhat at nursery, and so I did. I was three when I started at the Columbia Road Nursery, going there during school hours so that she could go back to work in the factory before collecting the boys and me. The nursery was lovely—black and white on the outside, with rooms decorated in red, blue and green, and kind, caring staff. I was happy, but even so I still had some fears. The worst thing was jumping off the wooden boxes there, which we used to do as a little ritual at the end of each day. I thought the boxes were huge and it took some persuasion to make me jump, but once I'd done it I was fine. Almost twenty years later my son Charley went there, and I was amazed to see how small those wooden boxes really were!

Occasionally on sunny Sundays a whole big gang of us, my parents' friends and their children would leave the East End behind and take a picnic to Teddington, beside the Thames, where we spent the afternoon playing games in the park. Mum and Dad had discovered Teddington when they'd been on a 'country' ramble advertised in the London *Evening Standard*. They thought it was gorgeous and often took us back there, even though it was some distance from home. When I was four Mum took us a little further afield, on holiday to a caravan in Clacton with her friend Barbara and her two boys. That was my first holiday away from the East End. After that we'd sometimes go to Majorca in the summer with a few of Dad's cab driver friends and their families, including Larry, who had been best man at my parents' wedding, and his wife Sandra and their two girls Alison and Claire.

It was in Majorca, when I was five, that I nearly drowned. My brothers and their friends were jumping off the side of the pool into rubber rings, and even though I couldn't swim I decided to copy them. Of course, being smaller I shot through the ring and under the water. The pool was really busy, and for a few moments no one noticed me. I tried to shout, but the minute I opened my mouth I gulped water. I remember thinking, *This is it—I'm dying*, when one of the other kids saw me and jumped in to grab me. Mum laid me down at the side of the pool, banging my back to make me cough up the water I'd swallowed, and then took me back to the apartment. It was a scary experience and, like the memory of Mum's fight, stayed with me for a very long time and only added to my general fearfulness about life.

The September after that holiday I started at Columbia Road Primary School, at the other end of the street from the nursery and just a short walk from our flat. The school had one playground at the front and another at the back. I didn't mind going there because most of my friends from nursery started with me, but even so I found it scary once I was inside. The corridors, which were grey and cold, seemed so long: it felt as though I spent most of my time running along them from one staircase to another, to the classroom, the playground or the assembly hall. Sometimes I had to go along them in my vest and knickers for PE, and I was absolutely frozen. Nowadays kids don't have to wander around in those sorts of clothes, but we did. I had knickers with the days of the week printed on them, but I was always wearing the wrong ones—I used to feel embarrassed that Mum never gave me the right day's knickers. On one occasion I forgot my knickers completely and nearly died of shame when Mum burst through the door waving them. My humiliation was made far worse by the fact that she'd brought Friday's knickers and it was a Wednesday.

Not long after I started school my parents arranged to exchange their council flat for a three-bedroom house in nearby Baxendale Street. It belonged to a housing trust, but soon afterwards they were offered the chance to buy rather than rent it. They weren't sure whether to—no one in either family had a mortgage, which was something they knew nothing about and found quite alarming. But Farvy persuaded them to go ahead: Mum and Dad became proud home-owners and never regretted it.

It was just a little terraced house with an outside toilet and a small back garden, but it was a big step up for us. The place was, however, in a terrible state, and for the next six months my parents worked hard—with the help of family and friends—to do it up. At first we all lived upstairs while the living room and kitchen were being done. We'd all get into Mum and Dad's bed at seven in the evening and watch the telly, because there was nowhere else to sit. There was no heating, and for a while we went to bed in scarves and gloves. I remember the smell of the new plaster on the walls, and the excitement as each room was finished. A bathroom was put in at the back and the living room was knocked through to the back room to give us more space.

There was one tragedy during this time, though—our lovely red setter Sergeant, who'd been with us since I was born, ate some of the paint from used tins left out in the garden. It must have affected his brain, because he went mad and had to be put down. We were all heartbroken, but especially Harry, who had loved Sergeant dearly. After his death we got a cat and Mum called her Kate because she'd always loved the name. Kate was a beautiful tortoiseshell, but she got on my nerves because she often jumped on me and scratched me, and I was never as fond of her as I was of Sergeant.

By Christmas 1978 the work was finished and we were settled in our new home. We thought it was paradise—there was central heating and the whole house was newly decorated. Since this was the seventies everything was in dark colours—the front room was dark green and gold with a deep red velvet sofa—and we thought it was dead cool. Mine was the smallest bedroom, but to my mind it was massive. I couldn't believe it was all mine: everything was pink and it looked really pretty. The bed slotted into the wall and had pink gingham curtains either side as well as at the window—all made by Mum. And in our house it was definitely Mum who was in charge. She was the one who organized everything, made most of the decisions and ran our lives—or so it certainly seemed to us kids—while Dad was happy to retreat to his armchair with the paper or nip down to the pub with his mates.

My brothers, at now fourteen and twelve, were out with their mates most of the time; I, at a mere six and a half, was at home with Mum. But much as I loved spending time with her, I wanted to be more grown up like the boys. I longed to fly out of the door as they did, calling over their shoulders that they'd be back for tea at six, or even that they were staying over with friends. To be sure, I was too young to go about on my own—but there was something else, too.

Even though I'd long since outgrown nappies and was at school, I was still considered the baby of the family and I hated it. I'd got used to hearing people say, 'Don't talk about that in front of the baby.' They'd send me upstairs so that they could carry on their conversations in private, or nod knowingly at each other and change the subject. As I got older and began to realize that I was being left out I grew more and more fed up. Why couldn't I know? I wasn't a baby any longer—just the youngest in the family. But somehow the idea that they had to protect me from anything 'uncomfortable' stuck. I became determined to show them—my parents, grandparents and even brothers—that I wasn't a baby and that anything they could do, I could do too. I used to feel angry and tell myself, *They think I'm an idiot*. They didn't, of course—it was just that they had failed to notice—or perhaps just didn't went to acknowledge—that I wasn't a baby any more. But the funny thing is that over the next few years,

24

while they were so busy protecting me from what everyone else was doing, I was getting up to all sorts of stuff that they knew nothing about.

2

GINGERNUT

From the day I arrived at primary school I was bullied, and my red hair made me an instant target. Other kids have no idea how miserable it is to stand out from the crowd because of the colour of your hair, and then get picked on for it. Believe me, I'd have done anything to change my hair to brown, black or even mouse if I'd had the chance. It wasn't just my hair, though. The little dresses and outfits that Mum so lovingly made me—she could knock up an entire outfit in an evening, and often did— and which my grandmas cooed over, made me feel embarrassed. Even though the dresses were lovely I always felt I looked odd and different when, like all kids, I was desperate to blend in.

There were three or four bullies who would walk past me, pull horrible faces and sing, 'Gingernut fell in the cup, swallowed all the fishes up.' Or they'd get me up against a wall and say, 'We're going to fight you.' Sometimes they'd follow me on the three-minute walk from school to home, calling me names and hitting me with their bags. And several times I was attacked behind the bike shed at the back of the playground, where the teachers couldn't see what was going on.

Another reason why I was an easy target was my

fearfulness—I'd quake when I saw them coming, and they knew it. I arrived home in tears every other day. Mum was forever coming up to the school to talk to the teachers, but there wasn't much they could do. If they told the bullies off, all the kids would just laugh at me. Mum used to say to me, 'Why don't you stand up to them? You've got to toughen up', but I hadn't a clue how to do that—I just wanted them to stop. I thought Mum was so brave and confident and I wished I could be like her. She did her best to intimidate the bullies, warning them to leave me alone, but they just made sure they got me when there were no adults about. There was one girl, called Lisa Lewis, who was on my side, and if she happened to be around she would come and fight the bullies for me. She wasn't scared of them, so they left her alone.

One day the fire alarm went off at school and we all trooped into the playground. While we were lining up one of the bullies said, 'Do yer want a fight?' I felt as though the whole school was watching and I thought, *This is never going to end unless I do it*. So I said, 'OK', and we arranged to meet after school down a cobbled alley called Ezra Street. I went there alone, and terrified. I didn't stand a chance, and I knew it. But I had to go and at least try. It was probably the bravest thing I'd ever done. I walked down to Ezra Street with my heart in my mouth. When I got there the bully was there with her mates. We both piled in and she started beating me up, dragging me on to the floor and pulling my hair. Goodness knows how badly I'd have been hurt if Lisa's sister hadn't come along at that point. She saved me, pulling the bully off and taking me—tearful and dirty—back home, while the bullies laughed and called me a baby.

That was the worst thing they could have done. I was still the baby at home, and now I was a baby at school too. I wanted to show them all that I wasn't. I decided I'd fight my own battles, and from then on I stopped telling Mum about the bullying. I didn't want her coming to the school any more—it didn't help anyway, because the bullies just accused me of hiding behind my mum. What I really longed for was to get away from the kids who were making my life hell, and when I was six something happened which gave me the escape route I needed. It came about by chance, and it showed me a world I'd never heard of before but which I instantly wanted to be part of.

My brother Albert, who was then eleven, was keen on acting. One day Mum saw in the *Evening Standard* that there was going to be an open audition for children who wanted to join the chorus of Andrew Lloyd Webber and Tim Rice's musical *Joseph and the Amazing Technicolour Dreamcoat* at the Westminster Theatre. She read it out to us in the kitchen, and Albert immediately wanted to go along. They were looking for kids from the age of eight upwards, but Mum took me too because she had no one to leave me with that day.

The audition was held in the theatre itself. Mothers were asked to go away and have a coffee for a couple of hours and then come back for their children. Mum made to take me with her but I refused to go, hanging on to Albert's arm and begging to stay. She told me I was too young, but when I started crying one of the chaperones looking after the children asked if I'd like to stay and watch. She promised Mum she'd make sure I was OK, and then sat me on her knee. As I gazed around at the theatre I thought it was the most amazing place I'd ever seen.

There were dozens of children there and they were asked to go on stage in small groups and sing 'Hark the Herald Angels Sing'. The casting director went through each group tapping children on the head—if you got tapped, you were in. When Albert's group went on stage the casting director asked me if I'd like to go up there and sing with him. I was thrilled and stood beside him singing my heart out—it was one of my favourite carols, and because of all the time Farvy and I had spent listening to music I had developed a great ear and very good pitch—even at that age music lifted me up and made me feel good. Both Albert and I got tapped on the head, and at that point Mum came back in and asked what I was doing up on stage. 'I think she's just been given a part in the show!' the chaperone replied.

Albert and I were both put into the chorus, despite the fact that I was a couple of years younger than any other child in it. There was a hiccup, though—I had to have a performing licence, issued by the local council, and the producers weren't sure I'd get one as I was so young. They told Mum to bring me to all the rehearsals anyway, while they tried to sort it out. In the end the licence came though just in time for the first performance. I have no idea why they wanted me—I was just one of a large number of children there that day. But I was so grateful that they did, because being in the show saved me from many horrendous days at school.

Joseph opened at the end of November 1978, ran

for three months, and was then put on again for another three months a year later. At first the producers had wanted me to ride in the chariot beside the star of the show, Paul Jones (former lead singer of the hugely successful band Manfred Mann) when he came on at the end. But when we tried it for the first time I burst into tears, so the idea had to be dropped and I stayed with the rest of the children's chorus. The performances were divided up among three groups of us, because under a certain age you are only allowed by law to spend limited hours each week on stage. We didn't have any special costumes, just our own clothes, and I loved it—especially when it meant missing school, which we did for matinées. Chaperones—usually some of the mums—looked after us at the theatre. The adult cast were lovely—Leonard Whiting played the Pharaoh and Frank Ellis played Simeon, and along with Paul Jones they were always teasing and having fun with us.

Being the youngest child I was fussed over by cast, crew and chaperones, and I was so happy being the centre of attention. Dad used to drop us off in his cab and pick us up again afterwards. I can still remember coming round the bend of the road into the City and seeing the Thames with all the lights on either side—it looked so glamorous and beautiful. It was only a mile or two from Bethnal Green, but it felt like a different world.

The Irish Republican Army had waged a bombing campaign in mainland Britain a couple of years earlier and there were still regular bomb scares in London. Once the theatre had to be evacuated for this reason and we all came out and did the show in the street. The audience, and the

29

passers-by, were delighted.

My life alternated between normal schooldays—when the bullies were always waiting for me—and days when I left early, or even missed school altogether, to go to the theatre. On those days—normally three a week—I was spoiled rotten by everyone, sang my heart out and then basked in the applause at the end of the show—and to cap it all I got paid for it. Not hard to work out which of my two lives I preferred!

One day one of the chaperones told Mum about an after-school theatre class for kids which wasn't far from where we lived. 'Take your kids to Anna Scher,' she said. 'She's wonderful, it doesn't cost much, and if they want to act that's the place to go.' Mum went along to enrol us, but there was a long waiting list and she was told it would be two to three years before we could start. But she put our names down and in the meantime took me to tap dancing classes in a church hall in Bethnal Green. It was opposite a Wimpy restaurant and sometimes several of us kids would skip our tap lesson and get a burger instead. Mum would come back, none the wiser, to pick me up at the end of the class.

It had been a long-held dream of my dad's to give up the cabs and manage a pub, so, while I was still in *Joseph* when the opportunity came up to take over one just up the road from us he talked Mum into it. There's no doubt that she was reluctant, but by this time their marriage was in trouble and perhaps she felt that supporting Dad in fulfilling his dream would give it one last chance. I didn't know my parents' relationship was under strain because there was no obvious sign of it. I never heard them row, and to me things seemed the same as they'd always been. But slowly and surely they were growing apart. With Dad spending so much time either working or drinking with his mates, Mum, left at home, was feeling increasingly discontented.

Oblivious to the tensions behind the scenes, I rather liked the pub, which felt big and cold and fascinated me. It was called the Acorn and there was accommodation upstairs, which we only used at weekends. During the week Dad ran the place while Mum continued with her machining job. Then at weekends Mum would take us kids over to the pub and we'd stay upstairs while she helped Dad behind the bar. While we had the pub, we got another dog, a Doberman we called Max after the film *Mad Max* with Mel Gibson. Max—the dog, that is—was huge and scary and I couldn't handle him at all. I'm not sure anyone else could either, because he wasn't with us for long. I loved sitting with Steve, the DJ who played at the Acorn at weekends, and I often helped with the bottling up in the cellar. When I wasn't needed for some jobs or other I played on the Space Invaders machine in the public bar. I used to play for hours and became quite addicted to it, convinced I would win every time.

Cheryl Baker from the band Bucks Fizz was a friend of my parents and used to come into the pub quite often. I worshipped her and thought she was utterly gorgeous, embodying as she did everything I dreamed of—beauty, confidence and talent. She was in the pub, chatting, laughing and thanking everyone for their good wishes, the night before Bucks Fizz sang in the Eurovision Song Contest. When their song, 'Making Your Mind Up', won I

31

couldn't believe that we actually knew her. I had Bucks Fizz posters on my walls and went to all their concerts with my dad or my cousins. In fact I went to pop concerts whenever I got the chance—I also saw Dollar, Status Quo and David Essex, whom I thought was the world's top heart-throb. I cried at the end of his concert, overwhelmed by the excitement of seeing him and by all the applause. Watching these stars on stage transported me into a different, dazzling world, and perhaps because in my real world I was so timid I liked to imagine myself, glamorous and in control, up on a stage just like them.

The pub only lasted for a year. Far from saving my parents' marriage, it was the final nail in its coffin. Mum hated it: she felt bad about carting us off to the pub at weekends, and doing two jobs was too much for her. It became obvious that the whole thing was impossible and Dad reluctantly agreed to give it up and go back to driving a taxi. I was still ignorant of how bad things had become between my parents. Rather than rowing I think they just stopped talking, and although there must have been tension in the atmosphere I wasn't aware of it. As far as I knew, everything was fine. The discovery that it wasn't was a huge shock, and it came on the day my parents separated.

The previous night my brother Harry, who was then fifteen, had a party at our house. I was eight and really wanted to go—it was exciting and grown up, and I wanted to be allowed to join in. Mum wanted to let me stay up for a while but Dad ordered me off to bed, so Mum took me upstairs and I stomped into my pink bedroom in a sulk. I loved watching all the older girls at my brothers' parties, in their Pringle clothes and sling-back high heels. Some of them wore outfits they'd bought from Mum—she made leather and suede skirts and tops in soft pastel shades and the girls would come to the house for them. At these parties they wore tons of make-up—electric blue eye shadow and glossy red lipstick—with their hair in flicked fringes. I thought they were so cool. And then there was the funky music, records such as 'Mama Used to Say' by Junior and the Mary Jane Girls. I longed to be a part of it, and being sent up to bed like a toddler was awful.

The next morning I heard my parents in the kitchen arguing. This was extremely unusual—in fact it was probably the only time I ever heard them doing so. As I went downstairs, full of anxiety, I heard Mum smash a cup in the sink. I was now really alarmed, but when I went into the kitchen there was Dad eating breakfast and Mum cooking as if nothing had happened, although I could feel the tension like a taut wire between them. That afternoon, when I got home from school, Mum was waiting at home. She sat Albert and Harry and me down to tea at six as usual and told us that she and Dad were splitting up. In fact Dad had already moved out, to his mum's flat. She said they both still loved us and that we could see Dad whenever we liked.

I was so stunned I didn't know what to say. None of us did. We all just sat there and looked at one another. The boys probably knew more about it than I did, but I just couldn't take it in—why on earth would my parents split up? It seemed that one minute everything was all right and normal, the next my dad was gone. It sent a seismic shockwave right through our family, yet none of us said anything more. Mum didn't offer an explanation and we didn't ask for one. We just carried on as if nothing had happened, ate our tea and then I went out to play in the street with the other kids.

I couldn't wait to tell my friends. It sounds heartless to say I enjoyed the drama of having such a big thing to tell everyone, but of course I wasn't heartless at all—I just had no idea how to cope or what to do. So I tried to keep everything as it was, and just treated my parents' split like something happening on the telly—quite exciting, but not much to do with me. I think that's how I coped, with what was actually an enormous event. I had no idea why Dad had gone and in those days parents didn't think of discussing such matters with the kids—they made the decision and we got told and that was that. I tried to make sense of it all and, because I couldn't, for a long time I thought that Mum and Dad's break-up was my fault. I believed that if I hadn't asked to go to Harry's party they wouldn't have argued over it and they wouldn't have split up. In my eight-year-old mind it was that simple. I never told anyone what I secretly felt—as a family we didn't talk about feelings. Like most families round about, we just got on with life and muddled through, loving each other but without much idea of what was going on for anyone else and without ever really talking. Only years later did Mum explain that the main reason for her separation from Dad was that she saw so little of him: he was either working or in the pub. Dad's version was that he was 'never good enough'. I'm sure the truth was a mix of those and many other reasons.

I missed Dad, although the day-to-day routine of my life didn't change hugely. Dad had always worked long hours, so we were used to not having him around. But I was aware, as I'm sure we all were, that he wasn't just out at work or in the pub—he wouldn't be coming home at the end of the day, or sitting behind the paper in his armchair. Mum had always been the centre of my world, and she still was. She did her best to keep things just as they had been for the boys and me. And to a great extent she succeeded. But while outwardly things went on pretty much as before, inevitably we all changed. Harry felt he had to be the man of the family after Dad left. He was always a loving and protective older brother, and he tried hard to look out for me, and indeed for all of us, after the split. I'm sure Albert felt the shockwaves too. After Dad left he seemed to be always out with his mates and, as I later learned, it was around this time that he began getting seriously involved with drugs. As for me, I think I felt a deep sense of loss and of the world never being quite the same again. I became more insecure, more anxious and more fearful than ever.

For years afterwards I'd say—to other people and to myself, 'I'm OK about the split. It's fine as long as Mum and Dad are happier now.' But of course for a little girl your parents splitting up isn't fine at all—it changes your world irrevocably. It was just that for so long I didn't realize how deeply it had affected me. Looking back, I think that drink and drugs, which I started dabbling in not long after my parents' separation and continued at an ever-increasing pace for many years, was in part, at least, my way of keeping those painful, hurt, bewildered feelings deep down out of sight. Perhaps the years of using, the tears, the panic attacks and the breakdown I suffered in my twenties may have been connected to those uncomfortable and unfamiliar feelings of grief and loss surfacing and refusing to be pushed back down.

My mum always used to say, 'It doesn't all go in your boots', and I know now how true that is. While writing this book I've relived the toughest times in my life and it has sometimes sent me into a very dark place where I've felt depressed and alone. I don't regret that. It's given me the chance to get a much clearer picture of my life, to be totally honest with myself, to admit how I really did feel at those times and to clear away some of the cobwebs of the past.

On a practical level the new set-up was quite straightforward. My brothers were old enough to go round and see Dad at his new flat whenever they wanted, and I saw him most weeks, usually at my Auntie Helen's house. But mostly I was playing there with my cousins Amelia and Fenton, so I didn't actually get to spend much time with Dad. He'd be downstairs with Auntie Helen and I'd be upstairs play-fighting with my cousins, and then Dad would take me home in the cab.

While I settled fairly easily into a pattern of being at home with Mum or visiting Dad at Auntie Helen's, there were more difficult aspects to the divorce. I often felt torn between my parents and I tried desperately not to upset either of them. Mum would say, 'Ask your father to buy you some new shoes for school.' But I didn't want to ask, I wanted Mum to do it. And when I did pluck up the courage to say, 'Mum says I need some new shoes,' he'd reply, 'I can't buy them—I've got bills to pay.' It got to the point where I dreaded asking him for anything. If Mum told me to ask I'd sit in the back of the cab fighting back tears, so scared I could hardly breathe. I didn't want Dad to be angry that I'd asked, or Mum to be angry that he'd said no. I just wanted them to sort it out between them and leave me out of it, but I wasn't brave enough to say so. Mostly I just didn't ask Dad for whatever it was. I suppose it was easier to face Mum's 'Why didn't you ask' than Dad's 'No', which felt like such a rejection.

When I look back, I feel a lot of sadness about the way I missed out on my dad. He was—and is—a lovely man, but so distant that I never got the chance to feel really close to him, even before he left. I've always stayed in touch with him and I know he loves me and is proud of me, and that means a lot.

Only a few months after the split he met someone new. Marcelle, though British-born, was a US citizen as she had previously been married to an American. She had lived in Los Angeles, had two sons much older then Albert and Harry and she couldn't have been more different from Mum, so at first it wasn't easy to accept her. But she told all kinds of stories about America, which I loved, especially about her friend Henry Winkler, who starred as the Fonz—the coolest teenager on the planet—in the sitcom *Happy Days*. At that time every kid from eight to eighteen was glued to it once a week. Marcelle promised that I could meet Henry when she and Dad took me to America and I was wild with excitement, telling all my friends and promising to bring back his autograph.

It was much longer before Mum met someone special. In the early days she dated one or two men, but I didn't like them and secretly hoped they'd go away, no doubt wanting to keep Mum to myself. Perhaps Mum sensed this, or perhaps she didn't really like them either, because none of them lasted long. She spent a lot of time on her own, working, keeping the house running and looking after us, and it must have been tough.

While things at home were settling into a new pattern, at school I was still being bullied. One of the worst incidents happened around this time. By now, at the age of eight or so, we were all busy playing girlfriend and boyfriend and all the girls were vying for the best-looking boys. Of course, I didn't stand a chance—my 'boyfriend' was the poorest boy in the class, the one who came to school in second-hand clothes. The boy everyone wanted to go out with was Steven Scully, who had his pick of the best-looking girls in the school. One day one of the bullies came into the classroom while I was washing paint pots after class. She was unexpectedly friendly and told me that Steven wanted to go out with me. I didn't know whether to believe her, but hoped that maybe I was being accepted by the 'in' crowd at last. I told her I'd love to go out with him. Then all her friends ran in, laughing—they'd been listening from behind the door. They started jeering at me, 'What makes you think he'd want to go out with *you*? You're so ugly!' Then they ran off laughing. I felt utterly humiliated.

I began pretending to be sick, so that I wouldn't have to go to school. I would sneak down to the

38

kitchen early in the morning and chop up a carrot, then stick the bits in the toilet, put talc on my face and tell Mum I'd thrown up. I acted my heart out, and most of the time it worked. Mum would fuss over me and tell me to go back to bed, and inside I'd be breathing a sigh of relief that I didn't have to face the playground that day.

Outside school I had plenty of friends and there was no bullying. So, like my brothers before me, I spent a lot of time playing out in the streets with the local kids. In those days it wasn't unusual for children as young as six or seven to be out with their friends. Of course at that age we didn't go far from home—just around the block and not across any busy roads—but as we got older we went to the haunts that all the kids before us had already frequented, hanging around local flats and parks. I remember going down the street on my new roller skates, thinking I was flying. I loved those skates— they were metal with leather lace-up bits at the front, and you had to fit them to your feet by adjusting the nut on the side. It was great being with my friends, shouting out at neighbours and people we knew so that they'd chase us off and we could run away giggling. We got up to all sorts of naughty little pranks, like going down to the flats where my cousins lived, taking things out of one open bathroom window and then swapping them with stuff from someone else's bathroom further along the block. Or we'd make what we thought were hilarious phone calls to random numbers out of the phone book. 'I'm watching you!' I'd rasp in my most Mata Hari voice, until the voice on the other end told me to bugger off and slammed down the phone.

We had a wonderful sense of freedom that most kids now don't have. Everyone in the neighbourhood knew us, so Mum never needed to worry about where I was—someone would always look out for me. Adults didn't feel they had to entertain kids in those days—we just went out to play while the grown-ups got on with their own things. I'd disappear for a couple of hours, only running home for some money when I heard the chimes of the approaching ice-cream van. But alongside the freedom of being an East End kid, happily playing out on familiar turf, there were dangers that no one thought about so much in those days. From the age of eight I began experimenting with drink and cigarettes, and my Mum had no idea at all.

The drinking started with my aunties' parties. They'd have big, merry gatherings of friends and neighbours and of course there was plenty to drink. My cousins and I used to go upstairs to play while the adults talked and laughed downstairs. One of our games was collecting all the dregs from the glasses, mixing them together into a vile brew and then daring each other to drink it. I could never resist the dare and I remember swallowing half a glass of assorted wine, beer and goodness knows what else, then running to the bathroom to throw up. Afterwards I was dead pleased with myself that I'd drunk it. And although it had made me sick I'd enjoyed the brief buzz the alcohol gave me—so much that I was ready to play this dangerous game all over again.

It was the beginning of a pattern that was to continue throughout my teenage years—drinking always made me throw up, yet I went straight back for more, always believing that this time it was going to be different. I began smoking cigarettes around this time, too. I had a friend whose mum was a heavy smoker and there was always a big ashtray full of butts at her place. When her mum wasn't around we used to pick them out, straighten them and smoke them. We hated the taste, of course, but we felt grown up. And I never thought of smoking as bad—everyone I knew did it, including my older brothers, cousins and friends, and I couldn't wait to get started. How could I have known then that those childhood experiments would lead me directly to drugs that were far more serious, with appalling consequences?

3

STAGE-STRUCK

One afternoon Mum got a call to say that a couple of places had come up at the Anna Scher Theatre School—Albert and I could start the following week. We'd forgotten all about it—I was almost nine, and it had been two and a half years since she'd put our names down. 'Do you want to go?' Mum asked now. I wasn't sure. I didn't really know anything about it and felt very shy at the thought of going somewhere new, with people I didn't know. But I'd liked being in *Joseph* and thought more of that would be good. And Albert had said he was going, although as he was older we wouldn't be in the same class. So, after hesitating for a while, I said yes. My brother could go on his own for his six

41

o'clock class, but it would be a bit of a trek for Mum as far as I was concerned. She'd have to get me up to the school in time for my junior class at four-thirty, go home and then come back for me when the class ended at six—either that or find somewhere near by to hang about and wait. But she said that if I wanted to go we'd give it a try.

I was terribly nervous the first time. Mum had collected me from school, taken me home for a drink and a biscuit and then hurried me off to catch the bus up to Islington. The school, in a converted church in Barnsbury Road, had a brown wooden sign outside which said 'Anna Scher Theatre' in gold letters. Inside there was a small lobby—the foyer, they called it—with big swing doors, and on the left a table where a woman sat, who asked for your name. Through these doors was the huge room that doubled as classroom and theatre: all it contained were a few rows of chairs, then a wide expanse of floor. Along both sides of the floor were benches where we sat during classes when we watched other kids perform, and at the far end was a stage which was only used for formal performances.

I went through the double doors that first day and just stood there, because I didn't know anyone. There were about thirty kids milling around, most of them my age or a bit older. On the walls hung pictures of famous ex-pupils: Gary and Martin Kemp from Spandau Ballet, Linda Robson and Pauline Quirke whom I knew from teen TV shows (they had yet to make *Birds of a Feather*), Phil Daniels, who was Jimmy in *Quadrophenia* and many years later went on to play Kevin Wicks in *EastEnders*, and Dexter Fletcher who'd been

42

Babyface in the film of *Bugsy Malone*. I was amazed. Had those famous people really gone to this place when they were kids? Immediately I wanted to be up there on the wall with them—it was the most wonderful thing I could imagine.

Then Anna Scher came in. She was about the same age as my mum, small, dark and very slim, and she moved across the room as though she was gliding. Her long hair was held back by a hairband and she wore high heels and a knee-length pencil skirt. She looked different from anyone I'd ever seen before, and I thought she was weird but lovely. Her background, I discovered later, was Jewish-Irish, and she would tell us stories about her childhood in Ireland, where she learned tap dancing and was a child actress. She used to say that she never felt completely one thing or the other—Jewish or Irish. That first morning she said hello to me and from then on she knew my name, as she did every other child's.

There was a blackboard to one side, and on it was something that Anna said had been written by Oscar Wilde. I had never heard of him and had no idea what it meant, but I was soon to learn that there would be a different inspirational saying or quote on the board every week and we were expected to learn it. Anna would pick on someone each week, during class, to repeat the saying on the board without looking at it. On the walls, alongside the photos of former students and colourful posters, was a chart with what Anna called the essential ten Ps of acting—Punctuality + Purpose, Preparation + Productivity, Presentation + Perseverance, Practice + Play and Positivity + Pace.

The class began with warm-up exercises—we all bounded around the room to Mike Oldfield's 'Tubular Bells', 'I Never Promised You a Rose Garden' by Lynn Anderson and 'Silly Games' by Janet Kay. After that she got us to practise some tongue-twisters, like 'Betty bought a bit of butter but the butter Betty bought was bitter'. We all fell around laughing as we tried to say it. It took me a while to get it right, but when I did I felt a real sense of achievement. When that was over we got down to the real work—improvisation. All Anna's teaching was based on improvisation, as I was soon to learn. There were never any scripts—perhaps because some of the kids couldn't really read, but also because Anna wanted us all to act as naturally as possible. She got us to choose partners and then gave us a first line—something like 'I'm leaving' or 'I've got some bad news.' We had to go off with our partners and come up with a short piece to act out, based on the line she had given us. Or sometimes it was an object, or just an idea. Then Anna would pick people at random to show the class what they had come up with. We didn't sing or dance much— only the occasional song, something like 'Give Peace a Chance' which fitted Anna's philosophy. She was on a mission to help and heal the world and we all became drawn into it, developing insight and a much more caring attitude.

I was amazed by it all, and really happy from the start. There was no bullying at Anna's—the other kids were great, and when you first arrived a couple of them were given the job of looking after you and showing you the ropes. The girls who looked after me were lovely and I soon settled in. A few years later I was asked to look after another new girl, called Saffron Burrows: I told her she ought to become a supermodel. After a few weeks Albert left. At fourteen he thought he was too old for the classes—he felt silly acting and preferred to hang out with his mates, which was a shame because he was talented. But for me it was the beginning of a really good time in my life—something completely different from home and school, a world in which imagination made anything possible and I could become anyone I chose. I threw myself into the weekly improvisations, always hoping to be picked by Anna to perform in front of the other kids. And my confidence, which had been so battered by school, grew. Being able to learn in my own time and in a creative way, without the pressure of deadlines, suited me, as did Anna's spiritual approach to life. It was all wonderful and I soaked it up.

Anna was strict, however. We had to be on time for classes and weren't allowed to swear in our mini-plays unless we could show that it was relevant to the plot—which we usually managed to do. And when she demanded silence—for instance when a couple of kids were acting their scene in front of the rest of us—she would hiss fiercely at anyone who made a noise or created a distraction. But none of us minded her strictness: we respected her and we behaved. We knew that she cared about us and wanted to bring out the best in us.

Upstairs Anna and her husband Charles Verrall, who ran the school with her, had a theatrical agency, organizing acting work for the students. Casting directors would get in touch with her and come along to watch classes, looking for the children they wanted. Anna was very careful about what her children did—no one was allowed to appear in advertisements until they were older.

I didn't know it then, but Anna's venture—which she had started as an after-school class in a local school in 1968 and later moved into the church which the council converted for her—was known as Britain's least conventional theatre school. She and Charles were hugely hard-working, bringing acting classes to kids who could never have afforded to go to drama school. The school was run as a charity and the classes cost 40p a time when I went, but if you didn't have the money she wouldn't turn you away. Anna taught hundreds of kids a week and had a waiting list of five thousand more. Her unusual teaching methods, designed to include everyone no matter how young and no matter whether they could read or not, were very successful—so much so that she even taught children in Africa. Each year she would go out there, taking a couple of her students with her; I longed to go and to feel that I was doing something worthwhile, but I was never chosen.

Anna produced dozens of young TV stars, not only those whose photos were on the wall when I arrived but many more in the years after that. Their numbers included Gillian Taylforth, Susan Tully and Natalie Cassidy, all of whom became famous in *EastEnders*, and Kathy Burke who starred in *Scrubbers* and *Gimme Gimme* among many other productions. Anna kept everyone's feet on the ground, monitoring our successes, encouraging self-belief and offering advice and support. We all loved her, and I knew from the start that I would owe her a great debt of gratitude.

I was terribly sad to learn that, a few years

ago, she suffered a breakdown and was asked to leave her own school by the board she had appointed to help run it. Although many of her friends and former students supported her attempts to have this decision overturned, she never went back. Being Anna—irrepressible, passionate and inspirational—she simply started a new school, calling it Anna in Exile, in a church near by, and as far as I know it's still going strong, as is the original Anna Scher Theatre.

When I was ten I got my first job through Anna: singing in a children's choir on a Pink Floyd video for a song called 'Bring the Boys Back Home' on their album *The Wall*. I knew Pink Floyd because their music was played at home, and my brothers and I were in awe of them. Soon after that my first real acting job came along. If you were going to be considered for a part when a casting director arrived, Anna would write your name on the board. I was thrilled to find mine there when a casting director for the TV detective drama *The Gentle Touch* arrived to find a couple of children for a small part in one episode. I acted my heart out as we went though our paces and was delighted to see the casting director watching me and making notes on his pad—I felt so important. I was called out, along with a few other children, to go to the coffee bar downstairs to read for him. When Anna rang a few days later to say I'd got the part I couldn't wait to tell my family. They were all thrilled—'Imagine little Julie on the telly,' my grandma Norah kept saying.

Just before I started, Anna rang my mum to say there was a problem—I was called Julie Harris and there was already another actress with that name, so if I was to work professionally I would have to have a stage name. I wasn't there at the time, so Mum said she'd talk to me about it. But Anna was in a hurry and urged her to think of something there and then. They mulled over a few names and then Anna asked, 'What's *your* name?'

'Pat,' my mum replied. 'My maiden name was Pat Palmer.'

'Perfect,' Anna said. 'That's what we'll call her— Patsy Palmer.'

That's how I came to be called by my mum's name, without knowing anything about it. I liked the name, but when I grew older I wished I'd been given the chance to choose one for myself.

A couple of weeks later I was taken to the BBC studios with my friend PJ, who was going to be in this episode too. I was excited about meeting the show's star, Jill Gascoyne, but I wasn't nervous about acting or being filmed. That part was easy—I just did as I was asked. We played a couple of kids who broke into a flat to kidnap a little girl who was being abused. The whole thing was great—we were having brilliant fun while everyone else was at school, and we got to be on the telly too.

It was around this time, when I was ten, that the promised holiday to America with Dad and Marcelle came about. I was wild with excitement about finally getting to meet the Fonz, but there was a shock in store. On the plane, Dad and Marcelle told me that they were getting married and were taking me over to be a bridesmaid. I had no time to get used to the idea and felt terribly upset. Why hadn't I been told before? And why weren't my brothers there too? Apparently Dad couldn't afford to take them as well, but to me it didn't make sense and I went through the wedding in a daze. I didn't really mind them marrying—Marcelle was nice and Dad was happy. But the way it happened seemed all wrong. And worst of all, I never got to meet Henry Winkler—it turned out that he was away while we were in the States. When I got back I lied to all my friends and said I'd met him—I was so convincing that I began to believe the lie myself.

When I was twelve Dad and Marcelle went to live in Los Angeles, and stayed there for the next six years. He went from being in my life, albeit on the fringes, to being almost totally out of it. I didn't fly over to visit him because there wasn't enough money. So almost overnight he was gone, and it seemed that all I had was Mum. For her, life was tough. Not only did she have a mortgage and three kids, but her parents were becoming more needy. Nor still popped in most days, but by the time I was eleven Farvy was too unwell to get out much. Mum and I used to go over to see him and run errands for him, and sometimes I'd help him make his way slowly and painfully over to our house for a visit. But although we still had a great laugh together and I was always the apple of his eye, it was clear that he would soon be housebound and that he and Nor would need an increasing amount of help.

I often worried about Mum. I had a picture of her that had been taken at work as she sat behind her sewing machine, and the expression on her face was thoughtful and sad. Whenever I looked at that picture I burst into tears. I wanted to protect Mum and make everything all right for her, but I couldn't. Instead I threw myself into my new passion for acting. It was wonderful to go to Anna's

49

and play the part of someone else—someone with a completely different life.

Plenty of famous actors, directors and writers came to visit the school, to offer their support for what Anna was doing, and I was always in awe of them. I remember Michael Caine, already a famous film actor best known for his role in *Alfie*, arriving for Anna's Festival of Plays. Director Alan Parker came at that time too, along with Martin Luther King's daughter, as did Eddie Kulukundis, the impresario husband of Susan Hampshire. The festival was held every summer and was the biggest event in the calendar.

Throughout the year students from each class would be chosen to direct a twenty-minute play. If you were a director you got to write the script, choose the cast and stage the whole play, which meant organizing lights, music and costumes as well as directing the actors. The plays were performed in front of three people in the class, who had been elected as adjudicators, plus Anna and Charles. The best ones were then put forward for the Festival of Plays and performed to an audience of students, families and visiting actors and casting directors. A winning play would be chosen, and the director was awarded a prize of a framed poem.

When I was twelve I was chosen to be a director. I was thrilled. At the time I really loved Randy Crawford's song 'Street Life', so I used that as my theme and wrote a play about prostitutes. It was a very dark play for a twelve-year-old, but a lot of our plays were then. I was in it, along with three friends. We rehearsed in the coffee bar in the basement of the theatre school, and when we performed it in the theatre the adjudicators chose it for the Festival of Plays. I couldn't believe it—my play!

That year there were five or six short plays in the Festival. My mum came to watch, and neither of us could believe it when mine won. Anna presented me with a framed copy of a poem called 'First They Came for the Jews' by Pastor Martin Niemöller, who opposed Hitler and was sent to a concentration camp. I had never achieved anything special at school, or stood out in any way, so winning the prize for best play at Anna Scher's made me feel special and clever in a way that nothing ever had before. The poem was wonderful and I treasured it for many years; I still remember the powerful effect its message had on me:

> First they came for the Jews
> And I did not speak out
> Because I was not a Jew.
> Then they came for the Communists
> And I did not speak out
> Because I was not a Communist.
> Then they came for the trade unionists
> And I did not speak out
> Because I was not a trade unionist.
> Then they came for me
> And there was no one left
> To speak out for me.

I made a lot of friends over the thirteen years during which I went to Anna's. It was there, soon after I arrived, that I met Sid Owen, who became one of my best friends and would later play my husband Ricky in *EastEnders*. We were both eight when we met—Sid is four months older than me—

and we liked each other straightaway. In many ways we were very similar. Sid was shy and timid, like me, and he loved to giggle—also like me. So we would try to make each other laugh.

His big brother, Mark, was a friend of my brother Albert, so by the time we were ten or eleven we were hanging around together a lot, playing, larking about or going to the cinema. After classes at Anna Scher's, we used to go to the adventure playground over the road, and smoke and drink—whenever we could sneak a cigarette or some alcohol. When we were eleven Sid was going out with my friend Jane Bristow, while I was going out with another boy from our acting class, John Alford, who later starred as a fire-fighter in the TV drama *London's Burning*. We all used to hang out at Islington Youth Centre, which was near the theatre school, or go to the pictures together.

One day the four of us plus some other friends decided to go to Margate for a day at the seaside on our own. We told our parents we were going with the workers from the Youth Centre and persuaded them that we were being met on the station platform. The parents couldn't get on to the platform without tickets, so they let us go through and we kids jumped on the train together, falling about laughing at our cleverness in pulling it off. We were all into Benetton clothes then—we wore Benetton rugby tops and cords (mine were pink) with Nike trainers. On the train the boys got into a fight with another crowd of lads, while we girls watched and shouted at them to stop. Luckily it wasn't too serious and no one was hurt, and when we got to Margate we had a fantastic day, going to the funfair and eating candyfloss and ice cream.

Our parents never did find out that we went on our own—the acting classes must have turned us into amazing little liars!

At the age of eleven I moved from primary school to Haggerston School for Girls in Hackney, a ten-minute walk from our house. On my first day I arrived in the playground kitted out in the smart grey uniform Mum had taken me to buy the week before. I'd never had school uniform before—at primary school we wore our own clothes—so I felt odd and stiff in my skirt, blouse and cardigan, with my new shoes shining. I hated the look of the place, which was huge and ugly like a prison. My teacher, a Miss Lambert, seemed nice, but I knew I wasn't going to like being there.

Lots of the girls from my old school were there, including the bullies. But I'd made a decision that I wasn't going to be bullied at secondary school: from now on it was going to be different. From the first day I acted with a confidence I didn't really feel—I laughed, joked around and made sure I had friends. And the bullies left me alone. It taught me that being the joker worked as a way to protect myself. That apart, I never really took school seriously. It was somewhere I had to go each day, so I went—but once there I just fooled around with my friends, sat bored out of my head in lessons and did as little work as possible, which was often none. Looking back, I feel sad about my lack of education and wish I'd studied. The teachers at my primary school had told Mum I was bright and could do well, but it didn't occur to me or any of my friends to try hard.

I think I had a few problems which didn't help. I had real difficulty concentrating, and I've since wondered whether I might have been suffering from Attention Deficit Disorder. On top of this I was dyslexic with numbers—I just couldn't make head or tail of them, so maths was something I dreaded. The maths teacher was a really cool guy who used to bring in albums to play to us and talked about music. I know it was his way of trying to get us kids interested, but although I liked him I got nowhere with the actual maths.

My friends and I used to joke about school—we called it Slaggerston, and were so brazen that we smoked out at the back of the school during playtime. Teachers occasionally saw us, but they did nothing. No doubt my problems in concentrating were made much worse by what I was getting up to outside school. By eleven I was regularly smoking cigarettes—we'd graduated to cadging fags from older kids and buying them from a local Indian shopkeeper called Terry who'd let us have a single cigarette for ten pence. But that was only the start—I'd begun smoking cannabis too. I knew my older brother smoked cannabis and hashish, which we all called puff or draw, and I couldn't wait to be like him. I thought my brother and his friends were so cool—anything they did I was desperate to do too.

Harry was a lot less wild than Albert, because after Dad left, being the oldest, he saw himself as the responsible one. He felt the burden of looking after the rest of us was on his shoulders, and did his best to watch out for us. I think he probably felt under a lot of pressure at the time. He worked incredibly hard. After he left school at fifteen he got a job as a builder and by seventeen he was studying for the Knowledge—he took it at eighteen, passed, and began to work, like his dad and grandad before him, in the honourable business of being a cabbie. Soon after that he moved into a flat with his girlfriend Vivien, who wore electric blue eye shadow and seemed to me the height of glamour. The flat was one that Norah rented from a housing association—for some reason she had this flat in her own name, even though she shared another with Farvy. Perhaps she used it to escape from him. If so, it was generous of her to pass it on to Harry and Viv, who later bought it outright.

Albert was very different. After Dad left he seemed to go wild, with the attitude that he could do anything he wanted. He was incredibly good-looking, and always surrounded by girls and mates, but by the age of fifteen he was taking heroin. I didn't know about this at first. Mum found out and was sick with worry: on top of everything else she was dealing with it was a huge blow. But she didn't tell me, because I was still only ten and she wanted to protect me. By the time I did find out, a year or so later, it was common knowledge. Someone told me when I was out playing, and suddenly I understood all the whispered conversations Mum had had with her parents and friends, all the worried frowns she wore and all the rows she had had with Albert, trying to keep him from going out. Once it had been so bad that she'd tried to tie him to a radiator to stop him leaving the house—she must have felt desperate.

I didn't let on to Mum that I knew—I used to say to my friends, 'Keep it quiet, but my brother's got a drug problem.' To me it was a bit of exciting news to share and I had no idea what it really meant, or of the desperation that both my parents must have felt at what was happening to Albert. But at the same time I could see changes in him that were frightening. He looked unkempt, pale and ill and sometimes he behaved oddly, laughing at things that weren't funny or lying around for hours, and I wished he'd just be normal again. I didn't like anything or anyone changing, and I could see that the changes in Albert weren't good. And I knew, even then, that I didn't want to be like him.

At sixteen he was sent to Ireland to stay with Dad's cousin Billy and become an apprentice, making fire-irons. Our parents hoped that if they got him away from the friends he was hanging out with, and the drugs, he could have a fresh start. There wasn't any rehab in those days, at least not in London's East End, so getting him away was the best they could come up with. Sadly, it didn't work. Albert stayed in Ireland a few months, but then came home and went straight back to his old ways.

Perhaps it wasn't surprising, given that drugs, and especially cannabis, were so easily available and considered 'normal' by so many of the kids I knew, that I began to experiment myself. In fact I couldn't wait to embark on this activity, which I saw as grown up, cool and independent. Albert used to have parties in our house with his mates when Mum was out. I would peep through the door at him and his friends smoking puff, think how nice it smelt and long to join in.

One day, when I was eleven, I found a small lump of hashish in the pocket of Albert's blazer. I broke a little bit off and ran to see one of my friends. Together we got some papers and a cigarette and rolled our first joint. It was a ham-fisted effort and it had us coughing and spluttering, but I felt really proud of myself. Soon after that I started to smoke puff regularly, and I was often stoned out of my head. I had plenty of friends who didn't do drugs, but I hung out most with the ones who did. We'd often make bongs—a kind of pipe made from an empty wine bottle half filled with water and a piece of grubby rubber tubing—and smoke that way. I'd arrive at school stoned and fall asleep in the classroom, have another session at lunchtime, then go and smoke again all evening.

Drugs were so easy to get hold of—everyone knew someone who would sell you a fiver's worth. I used to hand over my money to a Moroccan man in a café in Brick Lane, and in return he'd give me a little lump of dope wrapped in clingfilm. Getting hold of money wasn't too hard, either. I begged pocket money from Mum or my grandparents, and did odd jobs for family and neighbours.

My friends and I used to spend time in a place we called the Square—Fellows Court, off the Hackney Road. Albert's crowd used to hang out there, though by the time we arrived they had moved on to more exciting places like pubs and clubs. There were flats in the square and we'd cluster at the base of them, sitting on the concrete steps to chat and smoke our cigarettes and joints. We sat on those steps in rain, wind and snow, huddled against the cold, because we had nowhere else to go and we preferred to be there, away from adult eyes, than at home. Sometimes, though, I went round to my friend's house and we smoked puff when her mum was out. We used to do it in the bathroom, running the hot tap so that we could smoke in the steam, in case her mum came home unexpectedly.

Around the time I started smoking puff I began sniffing solvents too. Everyone was doing it. We'd sniff deodorants, correction fluid thinner— anything we could get our hands on that gave us a high and had us giggling and falling around the place, eyes glazed and totally spaced out. And on top of all this lot there was alcohol. I'd already been tipping back the dregs at my aunties' parties for a couple of years. Now I started on cider and bottled drinks, Thunderbirds and Pink Ladys, while we were hanging round the flats. I didn't get drunk—we always had to share what there was, so I never had enough, and anyway I was more interested in the puff. But if there was any booze going I'd always join in.

The drugs and the solvents and the drink made me feel so grown up, which I loved. I'd always been the baby in the family and I was so desperate to shake that off and show them all I could be just as grown up as they were. Being a shy child, I was very impressionable. I watched everyone around me, and took it all in, and decided very early on that being grown up would be a lot better than being a kid. And even though I wasn't bullied any more, the bullying had affected me deeply. Determined not to show my vulnerable side ever again, I laughed and joked and showed off and did everything the older kids did just as soon as I could, so that no one would ever pick on me again. Cigarettes, drugs and drink were my way of trying to be grown up. When I took them I felt more comfortable, part of everything, instead of left on the outside. I liked going round to my Auntie Amelia's house because all the kids were included in adult discussions there. They watched films like *Midnight Express* and *Papillon* and sat and talked a lot about life and politics and everything else, while Amelia produced huge pots of food. I envied them, because at home we didn't have the same sense of togetherness. My brothers were out a lot and Dad was gone, so often it was just me, with either Mum or Nor.

While I longed to have my brothers' freedom, I still felt babied. Most of my mates could stay out later than me; I had to be home by what I thought was a ridiculously early hour, and it just made me want to rebel more. Looking back, I can see that Mum felt very protective of me, the only girl in the family, and even more so after the divorce and Albert's problems. She was desperate to keep me away from drugs, but I thought she was just being mean.

I was careful not to let Mum find out what I was up to. I certainly didn't want to be grounded. If I was a bit stoned I always made sure I got home on time and then slipped straight up to my bedroom, just sticking my head round the living room door to call goodnight. I was really reckless, though, because sometimes I even smoked puff in my bedroom—I don't know what I'd have done if Mum had walked in. I can remember hearing her in the living room talking to a friend about Albert's drug problem and how worried she was—I just went up to my room and smoked a joint.

It wasn't that I didn't care. I did, very much. In fact I worried a lot about Mum and probably felt as protective of her as she did of me. If she cried I cried too, and when I saw that she was worried and anxious I would put my arms round her, wishing I could take it all away. When I went upstairs for a joint I didn't even make a connection between what I was doing and what Albert was doing. To me they were completely different. He had a drug problem, but I was just doing what all the kids were doing. I knew I shouldn't be doing it, though, and that was my little rebellion.

I used to say to my mates, 'Don't tell my big brother about this.' I idolized Harry, but I was a tiny bit scared of him too. He had lots of friends, but there was one I thought was really special. One afternoon I was in our kitchen with Mum when she said to me, 'Harry's got a friend who's absolutely gorgeous.' When the two of them arrived, I agreed. Richie, who was half-Spanish, was very good-looking. He was also very kind. Even though I was just a giggly, tongue-tied little girl, he always stopped to say hello to me. I often saw Richie with Harry and their other friend, Kevin—they were the same age and did the Knowledge together. Richie had a red VW Golf convertible—I thought it was so glamorous, and nearly died of joy when one day he offered to give me a ride round the block in it. I knew I was much too young for Richie, and felt sure that even if I wasn't he would never be interested in me because he was much too good-looking. I would never have believed it if I'd been told then that, almost twenty years later, I would marry him.

4

LITTLE GIRL LOST

A few months after I appeared in *The Gentle Touch* a producer came into our drama class looking for children to appear in the kids' drama series *Grange Hill*. We all loved *Grange Hill*, which had been running for six years and was set in a London comprehensive school. When I saw my name on the blackboard in the list of kids up for parts I was thrilled. After acting to my utmost ability in class that day I found I had been short-listed for the traditional second audition in the coffee bar. Anna carried on with the class while I and a few others trooped downstairs to read. Soon afterwards Anna phoned to say I had the part of Natasha and would begin filming in a couple of weeks.

I was in *Grange Hill* for most of the next three years, from 1984 to 1987. My boyfriend John Alford got a part too, which was great. When I say 'boyfriend', we were of course far too young for anything much to go on between us, but we hung about together for a few months and when we went to the cinema together we'd have a little kiss. John's was one of the main roles, while I was just an extra. I liked to call myself a main extra, though, because as well as being in the classroom or playground I got to say the odd line here and there. It was seldom more than 'Yes, miss', but I was quite happy—I got to be in the show, saw my name in the titles at the end and didn't have to learn any lines. I thought it was perfect.

Grange Hill was ground-breaking TV in its time, because it was the first realistic soap for kids. It dealt with truanting, bullying, smoking, drugs, shop-lifting, racism—in fact every taboo subject parents thought kids ought not to watch. But it always had a moral angle too. It managed to get a powerful message across in a really watchable programme, and I was proud to be part of it.

The Hill cast had included a lot of actors who later became very successful, including Todd Carty, Letitia Dean, Daniella Westbrook, Sean Maguire, Sue Tully, Sophie Lawrence and Michelle Gayle, all of whom went on to be in *EastEnders*. Of course they weren't all in it at the same time as me, but Sue Tully was and so was Sophie Lawrence, who played a girl in the same class.

On the days when I was filming I had to be dropped off about eight-thirty by Mum or Dad (before he went off to the States) at the Angel tube station, a couple of miles from our house, where the cast bus collected me. The bus would already contain thirty or forty kids, and but we still had to make a few more stops to pick up others before heading to the BBC's Wood Lane studios. On the bus I made friends with a girl called Dawn and we'd laugh and fool around and smoke behind the seats, trying to avoid the chaperones. They were lovely people, though—my favourite was Dexter Fletcher's nan. Dexter was another Anna Scher kid who had become famous in *Bugsy Malone* and went on to *Lock, Stock and Two Smoking Barrels*.

When we arrived we'd all head for the canteen, where every single morning I tucked into beans on toast, before going to the dressing rooms to put on our *Grange Hill* uniforms. After that we'd hang around until we were needed on set. When we spent the whole day there we had a tutor, who gave us three hours of tuition to make up for missing school. He was a lovely man, very funny and much nicer than any of my teachers at school. The rest of the time when we were waiting for our scenes we played pool or table tennis, went to the canteen for snacks or sneaked into the toilets to smoke.

After a year or so at Wood Lane, *Grange Hill* was moved to a new set in the BBC's Elstree studios. There was a much bigger, better set there, and a whole floor where we could spend time when we weren't needed on set. Not long after we got there they started shooting a new soap called *EastEnders*, which I watched because Sue Tully and Gilly Taylforth were in it. I didn't like it much—I was a bit too young for it—but my family and friends loved it, especially Dirty Den, the wicked, womanizing landlord of the Queen Vic pub, played by Leslie Grantham. We used to see him and the rest of the cast in the canteen, and one day Dawn and I plucked up courage to go and talk to him. He was lovely, and gave us his phone number so that we could prove to our friends that we'd really met him.

Top of the Pops was filmed at Elstree too, and we loved spotting the pop stars who were there to appear on it. One week we saw George Michael, already a huge success as half of Wham, with Andrew Ridgeley. We chased poor George all over the place trying to get his autograph, and must have driven him mad.

Most of the kids on *Grange Hill* came from Anna Scher's or the Sylvia Young Theatre School, and the two groups were deadly rivals. We called them slaggy, but actually the Sylvia Young kids could dance and sing and do all kinds of things, while we just swore and smoked and envied them like mad because they went to a proper theatre school. At least that's how we saw it then. Looking back, I realize that Anna Scher's gave us some fantastic preparation, not just for acting but for life. No matter how successful her pupils became, they were all very grounded. There were no bigheads at Anna's—you just got on with the job. I was never encouraged to be big-headed at home, either. My parents were proud that I was on TV, but after everyone had watched me a few times the fuss died down—after all, I wasn't actually *saying* anything on screen. Most of the time I didn't feel any different from my friends who weren't on TV. My school friends didn't make a big deal out of it either—they were used to me coming and going, and most of them were pleased for me. One or two of the older girls would say, 'Suppose you think you're something special', but I'd just say, 'No' and walk off.

Even though I had regular work on *Grange Hill* I wanted a Saturday job too. Most of my TV earnings Mum put away for me, and I wanted to earn some cash that I could go out and spend. I went up and down Bethnal Green Road, asking at all the market stalls and shops, and eventually I got a job in a butcher's shop. At eleven I wasn't legally allowed to work, but I knew the butcher and he agreed to let me help out on a Wednesday after school and a Saturday, for £5 a day. I felt very pleased with myself when I went home to tell Mum, but the reality wasn't quite so much fun. It was freezing in the back room of the shop, where I had to spend most of my time working the sausage machine. When I went home and held my hands over the fire Norah would say, 'Don't put 'em too close or you'll get chilblains.' I never did understand that. It was one of the many sayings that Norah and Mum had, like 'Eat your crusts and your hair will curl' or 'Eat ready-salted crisps to stop you burning in the sun.' Now I look back on these little sayings fondly, but at the time I thought they were mad.

When I was twelve Mum found herself a new boyfriend. His name was Ted Rice, and from the start I could tell she was serious about him. She'd been out with one or two men before, but they'd never lasted long and anyway I was jealous and didn't like any of them. But Ted was different. I knew he must be, because although Mum talked about seeing him she didn't bring him over to the house for ages. I think she wanted time to get to know him, without her kids' opinions spoiling things. Given his name I imagined him with a trilby hat and a moustache, a smooth operator with the gift of the gab. But when I finally met him, he was nothing like that. Shortish, with glasses and sandy hair, he had a warm smile and kind eyes.

It turned out that Mum had known Ted since she was young and had always thought he was really good-looking. Even though I was wary of him and not sure I was ready for her to have a serious boyfriend, I liked Ted straightaway. He was a friendly man who took an interest in me without talking down or patronizing me. He was also very generous, bringing presents for me every time he came to see Mum and treating her to lovely meals and evenings out. I could see that Ted was good for

65

her. She'd struggled along on her own for four years, worrying about all of us, trying to manage financially and juggling her job and family, and suddenly here was a man who offered to share all that and take some of the burden off her. I hoped he would stay around, and was glad when he did. He was always sensible and down to earth; with Ted there were no dramas—he was the one who calmed things down when they got heated.

However at the age I was I could be really stroppy, and although I liked Ted it didn't mean I was going to give him and Mum an easy time. I could be a nightmare, hurling myself on my bed in tears when I didn't get what I wanted. Ted had an apartment on Gran Canaria, where he took Mum and me for a holiday when I was thirteen. I was fed up because I didn't want to be there—I'd rather be at home with my mates. Mum and Ted had promised me it would be hot there, but when we arrived it was raining, and indeed it rained most of the week. I gave the two of them such a hard time, moaning and complaining, that Mum lost her temper and lashed out at me. She didn't hurt me, but I was shocked because she never did that sort of thing. I burst into tears, while she ran and locked herself in the bedroom. As for Ted, he just shrugged and laughed. He had a fantastically relaxed attitude, and it wasn't long before Mum and I had calmed down and made up.

Ted had been married before and had a son and daughter—Tracey and Tony—who were much older than me. He owned a video shop in Hoxton market, but he was also involved in all kinds of business dealings. After he moved in with us all kinds of things were brought into the house and taken out again—clothes, jewellery, gadgets and electrical equipment. It was all coming from somewhere and being sold somewhere else. That was common in the East End then—you'd buy something going cheap and sell it on to make a bit of a profit. Of course, a lot of the stuff was knocked off—though Ted's wasn't.

There was a funny kind of morality in the East End that said it was OK to steal from big organizations, companies or shops that wouldn't really miss it, but not from individuals. I feel bad when I think about it now, because I'm so careful to teach my kids that any kind of stealing is wrong, but as a kid I picked up the general attitude that there were some kinds of nicking that were all right.

In fact I did a bit of shop-lifting myself.

When I was twelve there was a school skiing trip I desperately wanted to go on, but I didn't have the right clothes. I went and nicked three tracksuits from C & A, and it gave me a real buzz when I got away with it. But my trail of crime came to an abrupt halt when I was caught nicking toys from Hamley's, the giant toy shop in London's Regent Street. I had taken Ted's grandson, four-year-old Ted junior, with me as cover and had stuffed an armload of toys under my coat, planning to sell them in the market for a bit of cash. As I walked out of the shop I felt a hand on my shoulder and I froze. I was taken up to the office, where I apologized and said I'd only done it for my little nephew; I was let off with a warning. It was enough to scare me and I decided shop-lifting just wasn't for me.

But while I was happy to give crime a miss after

this salutary experience, I was getting more and more deeply involved with drugs and alcohol. The only boundary I had was that I wouldn't take heroin—I saw what it was doing to Albert, who by this time was not only looking rough but stealing to feed his habit, and I didn't want that. My brother was getting into more and more trouble, and we all knew he'd end up in prison if he didn't watch out. The police had already knocked on our door several times to talk to Mum.

There were other incidents, too, such as the one when I was sitting watching a horror film—I think it was one of the *Halloween* films—on telly at Albert's girlfriend's house with her mum. Suddenly Albert and his girlfriend's brother flew into the house, ran upstairs, tore off their clothes and leaped into bed. A couple of minutes later the police arrived, looking for them. The girlfriend's mum swore they'd been in bed all along and the police let it go. One of them glanced at the film I was watching and said, 'Bit young for that, isn't she?' At the time I thought he was just interfering, but with hindsight he was probably right. I don't think Albert's girlfriend's mum thought there was any harm in it—a lot of adults weren't as cautious about such things then as they would be now.

On several occasions I was woken up by the police coming into my bedroom and tearing it apart, looking for drugs or stolen goods. They'd say, 'Sorry, love' as I stared, wide-eyed, from my pink bed. Then they'd disappear, leaving my things pulled out all over the room. Mum would always be downstairs crying, and that's what upset me. I didn't mind too much about my room, but I hated to see Mum in tears.

Heroin may have been out of bounds for me, but anything else was fine, which was why when my friend Barry offered me some cocaine I couldn't wait to try it. Still only thirteen, I was already keen to move on from puff and solvents to something more glamorous. I sniffed the cocaine eagerly, but felt very let down when it didn't seem to do much for me. I decided it wasn't so great after all, and didn't try it again for some time.

My next experiment was with LSD, known as acid, a hallucinogenic drug that I found far more exciting. I couldn't believe that the tablet Barry handed me, a tiny little thing called a black microdot, would do anything, but only minutes after taking it the effects kicked in and I was experiencing my first trip. The room began to swim around me, objects came to life and I felt as if I was outside my body. We went for a walk and the buildings around me appeared to come to life, while people in the street turned into weird creatures. I had no idea what I was doing or how long I would be in this altered world, wandering down the street, when suddenly a car drew up beside me. It was Ted's gold BMW and Mum and Ted were in the front. I stared at them. The car and Mum seemed enormous, while Ted had shrunk to a miniature person. They asked me where I was going, and my drugged brain screamed at me to seem normal so that they'd go away. I said the most normal thing I could think of: 'Got a fiver?' Ted handed me the money, and they said, 'See you later' and drove off. I almost collapsed with relief.

The trip went on for hours, and when I walked home later that evening I did everything I could to bring it to an end. I'd been told orange juice could help, so I drank loads, but that didn't work and eventually I resorted to sticking my fingers down my throat to make myself sick. I was in my Mum's bedroom, because by that time my little pink room had been turned into a bathroom and I was sharing a room with Albert. When he wanted to take his girlfriend in there I slept in Mum's room. On this particular night she was over at Ted's, which was just as well because I was sick all over the floor beside the bed. At that moment I heard Albert and his girlfriend arrive home in a taxi—which in my drugged state I thought was a fire engine. I climbed quickly into the bed and pretended to be asleep. Albert—who was supposed to be in charge while Mum was out—came in to check on me. Luckily the vomit was on the other side of the bed and he didn't see it, though I don't know how he could have ignored the smell. He leaned over and said, 'You all right, Julie?' and I murmured 'Yes', so he went next door with his girlfriend while I fell asleep, exhausted from both the trip and all the vomiting.

The next day I had to own up to Albert, and we cleaned up the mess in Mum's room. I promised myself I would never, ever take acid again. It had been a frightening experience, and I didn't feel normal again for a couple of days. I kept my promise for just two weeks, then decided to take just half a microdot so that I wouldn't have such a big trip. It didn't make a lot of difference, though— I was off my head again for hours, laughing like a madwoman.

By this time Mum was often staying over at Ted's. She was still worried sick about Albert, and Ted gave her a lot of support. Albert wasn't working, and Mum was afraid that he was being drawn deeper into the world of drugs and crime; I think she came close to a breakdown several times. She would leave me at home for the night, but only if a friend came to stay with me. I'd ask her if it would be OK to have a few more friends over for the evening. She'd say yes, thinking I meant one or two girlfriends for a cake-baking session. She had no idea I meant an all-night, all-out rave. The first time this happened I couldn't believe my luck, and invited everyone I knew. We all sat in the dark, listening to Pink Floyd, Led Zeppelin, U2 and Simple Minds, and getting stoned. But before long things escalated. Some of my friends had started taking heroin and they wanted to bring it to the parties, but I refused to let them into the house. It was hard to turn them away, but I knew how upset Mum was about Albert and I wasn't going to let anyone take heroin in our house and risk even more trouble for her. I know that if I'd given in and tried heroin myself I probably would have liked the effects and become hooked. I'm so grateful that I was too scared to try it on the few occasions when it was offered to me. Somehow in my mind heroin was bad and dangerous in a way that other drugs weren't. I knew heroin made you addicted, and I didn't think other drugs did—I still just thought of them as exciting, something to give me a buzz.

Albert used to come home while my friends were all there partying. I remember him asking me, 'Do you smoke now?' I hesitated, scared to say yes, when one of the boys said, 'You should see her have a bong.' Albert laughed, and after that I smoked puff in front of him. I knew he wouldn't say anything to Mum—he couldn't really, since he was so often out of his head on drugs too. There's no doubt in my mind that my family suffers from an addictive streak. We seem to be magnetically attracted to drink or drugs or both, and yet we can't handle them at all. I can remember Mum, on a number of occasions when she'd had a few drinks, with her head down the toilet. She was probably allergic to alcohol. And I was often sick too—more and more often, as I ignored my body's warning signs and kept taking the noxious substances that I was so drawn to.

While now I can look back and see that it was part of my struggle to feel as grown up as my brothers and to suppress all kinds of unspoken feelings, at the time I felt I was having loads of fun. My friends and I were all into it—though I was a lot worse than most of them—and we just thought it was a laugh. And when I was high everything seemed wonderful. I loved the feeling, and it was easy to get high as often as I wanted. Cost wasn't an issue, because amazingly I hardly ever had to pay for drugs. I paid for puff, but all the other drugs I took were given to me. There always seemed to be people around with loads of drugs, and as far as I was concerned they were as cheap and as easy to get hold of as Smarties.

Mum did her best to protect me. After what she'd been through with Albert she was terrified I'd fall prey to drugs too and wanted to keep me safely at home, but I fought her all the way. When she told me that I had to be home by quarter to nine at weekends while all my friends were out until ten it made me furious, and I threw all kinds of scenes to make her change her mind. I was very manipulative when it came to getting my own way about going out, or getting money. I'd be really nice and make her laugh, and if that didn't work I'd burst into tears.

I remember once I wanted to go to the pub with my friends. Mum said no—I was only thirteen, so it was perfectly reasonable for her to refuse—but I was determined. I lay on the sofa crying my eyes out. It's ironic that she thought I was too young, and that by crying like a baby I was proving her right. But I made such a fuss that in the end she agreed. I shot upstairs to get ready. I had recently permed my hair into a shoulder-length frizz—truly not a good look, though I thought it was brilliant at the time—and I decided to borrow some of Mum's clothes for the evening. I put on bright yellow ribbed leggings (this was the eighties, remember), a bright yellow top with shoulder pads (ouch) and bright red lipstick. I must have looked like a demented canary. It was my first official visit to a pub, though I'd sneaked in a few times before, and I wanted to look the part.

When we got there my friends were all drinking Martini and lemonade, which I couldn't wait to try. I thought it was lovely, as was Southern Comfort—our other favourite pub drink. By this time we were beginning to get seriously interested in boys. In the pub that night there was one called Lenny whom I really fancied. He was tall, blond and had what we thought was a bit of a funny accent—Liverpudlian with Cockney on top. I thought it was cute and I loved the way his hair fell in a wedge over his eyes. Lenny didn't fancy me in the least—which didn't stop me hanging around him, hoping he'd change his mind. I became obsessed with him, something that was to become a pattern with me. I would eat, sleep and breathe the boy I fancied, and if he didn't fancy me back it only made me want him more.

I bumped back down to earth when he asked my friend Toni out. She did so without telling me, and I was heartbroken when I found out. It didn't last long, though. They broke up, Toni started to go out with an older boy, and eventually my chance with Lenny arrived. We were all partying at my house, and Toni and her boyfriend were in one room while Lenny and I were in another. I was stoned and he had just started using heroin, so he was in a worse state than I was. He kissed me and I began to think, *I've got my dream.* But somehow it wasn't the dream I'd imagined. We were both so out of it that we barely knew what we were doing. Lenny began to undress, and I thought, *If I take my clothes off, maybe he'll want to go out with me. Is this what people do?* We both ended up naked, but it was awkward and uncomfortable and neither of us was sure what to do. We got dressed again and after that, whether through embarrassment or contempt, Lenny didn't speak to me at all.

Most of my friends had older brothers and we were all doing our best to follow in their footsteps. By the age of thirteen we'd moved on from hanging around the flats on a Saturday night to going to pubs along the Hackney Road. The pubs where we went had been buzzing when our brothers went there a few years earlier and we were trying hard to re-create the excitement, which had often included fights with bar stools flying through the air.

Once I began going to pubs there was no going back—I was sucked into the alcohol culture and I loved it. I'd spend the night at my friends' houses rather than go home afterwards, because I was in such a state. I was still smoking puff, and the combination of the drug with alcohol in my thirteen-year-old system was horrendous. Being violently sick—which I always was—never put me off. I just thought of it as something that happened, ignored it and went on drinking and smoking.

Around this time I discovered yet another drug—Speed. Someone's older brother or sister gave it to me. Speed is an amphetamine, a stimulant drug, like cocaine. I hated the foul taste of the powder, which had to be taken neat or mixed into a drink, but I loved the effect. Speed makes you feel wide awake and chatty. You can dance all night—in fact you can't keep still. Not only did it get me high, but I found that on Speed I could drink more alcohol without getting sick and I didn't need to waste time eating, because it killed my appetite stone dead.

I feel sad when I think of the way I was at thirteen—still—a child, yet doing things no child should ever do. On a typical day I got out of bed, put my uniform on, left home with no breakfast, walked to the flats to meet my friend, smoked a joint, then went to school already stoned. My first meal would be school dinner, then afterwards we'd go out to the back where teachers never went and smoke some more puff. Sometimes we sneaked out to a friend's flat in a rundown block near by, creeping in past his mum and sitting in his room smoking puff through a bong. Smoking that way intensified the effect, and as we watched the water in the bottle turn black from the smoke I used to get so stoned that I fell asleep and had to be woken up to get back to school for afternoon lessons. After school we'd go home for tea and then a big gang of us would meet up and hang around the Square or the flats, smoking and drinking. We'd stay there as long as we could before going home to bed.

I was still a little girl in so many ways, yet I thought I knew it all.

5

BOYFRIENDS

By the age of fourteen I was convinced that if only I had a boyfriend and could be half of a couple, everything in my life would be all right. It wasn't that I felt aware of anything being obviously wrong, just that I craved love and security. And while I didn't think my life was any different from my friends', looking back I can see that there were obvious reasons for my insecurity.

By this time Dad had been living in Los Angeles for a couple of years, working as a plumber. Ted offered to pay for me to go and visit him, but Dad said he hadn't got room where he and Marcelle were living. That hurt. I couldn't help feeling that he had a new life now and didn't really want me.

Albert was already in and out of prison for theft. He was stealing to feed his drug habit and was always either on the run or inside. We were all relieved in a way when he went inside, because we knew he would find it a lot harder to get drugs there and hoped it would give him a chance to clean up. It never did, though, because he was never inside for very long, and in any case he often managed to get hold of drugs in prison.

Harry was living with his girlfriend and working as a cabbie, and I didn't see a lot of him. I knew he was there for me if I needed him, and I used to go round to their flat and see them. But he had his own life. So I was at home with Mum, and sometimes on my own, when she was at Ted's. Mum was as loving as any mother could be. She cared, and she showed me that she cared, talking to me, giving me hugs and being there for me. But what I really needed was a close family who talked to each other and spent time together. And if I couldn't find that, what I wanted was a boyfriend.

After the fiasco with Lenny, it wasn't long before I spotted another boy of my dreams. He was called Bernard Bristow, and I was fourteen when I met him on the dance floor of a pub where we were both drinking with our friends. The moment I saw him I fancied him and decided he had to be my boyfriend, and from then on I was desperate to do anything to win him. I hadn't a clue what a relationship was really about or even what he was really like—I just wanted a boyfriend and, on the basis of a two-minute chat, decided he fitted the bill. We had a dance that night and the next week, when I went back to the pub with my friends, he was there again with his mates, who were all several years older than us. A few of my girlfriends fancied his friends, and one couple started going out together. This gave me the opportunity to hang around him a lot more, and eventually he and I got together. I think Bernard was more than a little reluctant, but he was a nice boy and probably felt sorry for me. He used to run away from me and my mates would say, 'Isn't it obvious he doesn't want you?' But I just wouldn't listen—I wanted to believe that he liked me.

He was nineteen, five years older than me, and I'm sure he'd have preferred to go out with a girl his own age. But I was convinced we were perfect for one another and followed him round like a puppy. We did get on well, especially when we were alone, when we'd talk for hours. Although we never did more than kiss I would sometimes stay at his house for the night after going to the pub, telling Mum I was with a girlfriend.

When I did tell Mum I had a boyfriend she wasn't too happy as I was so young. She said she wanted to meet him, so I brought him to Ted's daughter's engagement party at our house. I felt really grown up bringing Bernard, who was very polite and impressed Mum and Ted. But inevitably the romance, having never truly got off the ground, was doomed. I saw him for a few months before the penny dropped that he really didn't want to go out with me.

Soon after I broke up—or perhaps faded out would be more apt—with Bernard I was mugged in the street. It was a truly awful experience, which left me deeply shocked and frightened. Ted had given me a gold chain-link Krugerrand necklace for my fourteenth birthday. I thought it was wonderful and wore it to school every day under my uniform. I had shown it off to all my friends, so everyone knew about it. On the day of the attack I was walking along the Hackney Road with my friend Toni, wearing my necklace under my uniform as usual, and some gold rings—we all loved gold and wore as much of it as we could get. It was four in the afternoon and there were plenty of people around, so when two big scary-looking teenage boys walked past us we weren't worried. One of them asked us if we had the time and we said no, sorry, we didn't. They looked about seventeen and walked with a swagger—the kind of big, muscular guys who liked to appear intimidating.

A moment later one of them ran at me and knocked me to the ground. He got on top of me, holding me down, shouting that my mother was a whore and groping my breasts. I remember feeling violated and terrified about what he would do next. Toni screamed and jumped on his back, trying to get him off me. I yelled at her to get off him, in case he had a knife. The other boy was just standing by, not doing a thing, perhaps so that passers-by would think it was just a bit of fun. The guy on top of me pulled open the neck of my school shirt, grabbed my gold chain, got off me and ran. By this time people in the vicinity had realized what was happening and a man from a nearby garage chased the boys. Someone called the police, who came and took us home. I was in shock, shaking and crying. What scared me was that the boys had known I was wearing the chain. It was hidden under my clothes, yet it was the only thing they took. Someone had told them about it and set me up.

Albert was at home, and when he heard what had happened he grabbed a couple of his mates and went straight out to look for the muggers. The joke was that he shot off so fast he forgot to ask me what they looked like. Despite the state I was in I couldn't help laughing with Toni—we knew the boys would soon have to come back.

Mum wasn't yet home from work, and I knew

that when she got back and heard what had happened she'd be horrified and want to comfort me. If I'd waited for her it might have helped me to feel better, but I didn't. Instead, I went round to a friend's house and smoked some puff—my way of escaping the feelings of fear and shock.

Soon afterwards the police found the muggers. They wanted me to attend an identity parade, but I wouldn't go and pick them out because I was terrified that if I did they'd kill me. The whole incident left me very shaken, and even today I still get scared if a big or menacing-looking man comes close to me in the street.

There was a culture of violence in the area where I grew up which was shocking and frightening, but which most people took for granted. Violence was an everyday thing, and it touched my life in many ways. I remember being round at someone's house with a bunch of kids my age when a boy I knew walked into the house and stabbed another boy who was sitting a couple of feet from me—it seemed they'd had an argument earlier that day. The boy who'd done it then spotted me and said, 'All right, Ju?' before strolling out again, leaving his victim writhing in agony. Luckily the wound was in his leg and not life-threatening, but I was horrified.

One of the places I used to go to was a pub near home called Jazzy Dee's. I often went there with friends, and sometimes on Sunday lunchtimes I went on my own. A band called the Raving Jekyls used to play there and I thought they were really good, so I'd turn up to watch them and see who else was around.

One Sunday I saw a boy called Danny there. I

didn't know him, but I knew who he was—I'd first seen him in a photo that one of the girls was showing round school a couple of years earlier. The picture was of a group of older boys, and we all giggled and pointed out the ones we fancied. For me, Danny stood out straightaway. It wasn't that I fancied him—more that he had a wild look in his eyes that both disturbed and attracted me. When I asked who he was my friends said, 'Oh, him? He's mad!' Now here he was in Jazzy Dee's, and we got talking.

I already knew that he had loads of girlfriends and didn't seem to care about any of them. Whenever I'd seen him in the past they'd been crowding round him. He also drank a lot, took drugs like so many of us, and had a reputation as a fighter—it wasn't unusual for his nights out to end with either him or another guy flat on the floor. I'd been warned to stay away from him by lots of people who had told me he wasn't good news. But all this just encouraged me. I was always attracted to older boys, which I guess was all part of me trying to be more grown up.

That Sunday he kept whispering in my ear, 'You're really gorgeous.' That was enough to get me well and truly hooked. By the time I went home I couldn't wait to see him again. My obsessions with Lenny and Bernard were just warm-ups for the way I felt and behaved with Danny. Within days I was thinking about him all the time, plotting to be the only girl in his life and certain that I could make him love me.

At first Danny thought of me as no more than a kid and took very little notice of me. But I was so determined to be with him that after a while he began to hang about with me. We weren't exactly dating, but we did see each other. I told my friends we had 'a little thing going'. What that meant in reality was that when Danny had nothing better to do he'd see me, and we'd talk, drink, flirt and share a few kisses. If anyone had asked him if he was going out with me he'd have laughed. If they'd asked me, I'd have said I was. I convinced myself he was my boyfriend and told my friends he was, even though they pointed out that he was regularly seen around with other girls and didn't act in the least like a boyfriend. From the start he often rejected and humiliated me. When he couldn't be bothered with me he'd ignore me, or even insult me and tell me to get lost. But he kept me on a line and he knew just how to reel me in and how to keep me hanging around, wanting more. He'd suddenly be interested and attentive, standing with his arm possessively round me. He'd make me laugh, tell me I was lovely and insist I was his girl, even though we both knew he had plenty of other girls. If I said anything about them he'd deny seeing anyone else and insist I was special to him. I'd go home on a cloud of happiness, only to find him ignoring me again the next day.

Danny could be funny and great company, or vicious and cruel. He was totally unpredictable, a loose cannon who could suddenly appear from nowhere or disappear for hours or days at a time. I'd be in a pub with him and he'd say, 'I'm just going out to make a call.' I'd sit there for a couple of hours, waiting for him to come back, before it dawned on me that he wasn't going to. Sometimes I'd find him later at a party at someone's house, but if I said, 'Where were you? Where did you go?'

he'd tell me to go away and stop bothering him.

I don't blame Danny for the way he was, because I could have walked away and yet I didn't. If I'd understood anything about self-respect, dignity or real, loving relationships I'd have run a mile from him. But I didn't have a clue, and Danny became the latest focus of my obsessive behaviour. He probably couldn't have shaken me off even if he'd tried.

By this time I was a real party girl. With my group of girlfriends I hung around trendy pubs in Islington and went to Camden Palace on Wednesday nights, where the bouncer, Lenny McLean, who later wrote the best-selling book *The Governor*, let us in for free. On Thursday nights we used to go to a club in Charing Cross called the Future. I loved the nightclub scene, which made me feel excited and alive. The music was loud, the clubs were packed with people dressed in wild outfits, and I just wanted to be part of it all. Danny was sometimes in these places with his friends, and every time I hoped it would be a lucky night for me and that he would turn up, be nice to me and treat me like his girlfriend.

It was on the club scene, when I was fifteen, that I discovered the drug that topped all the others— Ecstasy. I can't remember who first gave it to me, only the unbelievable high it gave me—the fabulous feeling that I could do anything and live for ever. Even the dreadful sickness it brought on wasn't enough to put me off. I sometimes threw up in the middle of the dance floor, but I'd still go back and take some more. I had absolutely no idea of the harm, both real and potential, that I was doing to myself.

In all the clubs and pubs we saw a lot of the same faces, many of them people from our neck of the woods. Richie, Harry's friend, was one of them. He'd be there with his friends and I'd be with mine and we often ended up in the same crowd for the evening. But I still felt he was out of my league. There was something about Richie that I longed for but at the same time scared me, and that was how normal and down to earth he was. He liked to go out and have a good time, but he knew when he'd had enough and he always went back home. He had a strong, loving family and he liked to be with them; he enjoyed his nan's roast on a Sunday and got on well with his two sisters. I longed for what he had, but for me it was so different. I never wanted to go home, just to party all night and all the next day. It wasn't that I didn't want to see my family, because I loved them to bits. But I would have given anything to have that regular family togetherness that Richie enjoyed, with big family gatherings and dinners.

In addition, of course, I was in the grip of addiction and that came before anything else. I didn't think I was an addict—I thought I was just a party girl having fun, and that I could take it or leave it. But I know now that wasn't the truth at all. I am an addictive person and I was taking drugs not for pleasure, but in a desperate, compulsive and self-destructive way. I was so young, yet no one was in a position to step in and help me, to try to stop me. My family didn't know, and my friends—many of whom were taking drugs themselves—didn't understand how serious it was. They did try to stop me when I'd really gone too far. At the stage where I was being sick on the dance floor and then begging for more Ecstasy they told me I shouldn't. But I shook them off and insisted I was fine, then carried on taking drugs, being sick, staggering back to someone's house to sleep it off and then getting up to take more drugs.

When I was really high my left eye used to go all wonky. My friends thought it was hilarious, and said, 'Julie, sort your eye out!' I'd peer into the mirror in the loo and see how weird it looked, but I didn't care. As far as I was concerned I was having a wonderful time. And no one, not even those friends who begged me to stop, could persuade me otherwise.

Nothing illustrates more clearly the grip that drugs now had on me than the way I behaved when my beloved nan, Norah, died. It's a time I think back to with a lot of sadness. Ted had given me a job in his video shop in Hoxton market, where I worked on weekends and in the holidays. Two older girls worked there too—Tracey, Ted's daughter, and Joanne, who was Richie's cousin. Tracey and Joanne used to take turns buying the cigarettes every morning before work. There was a little fire in the shop, one of those free-standing Calor gas ones with a grille in front. You had to be standing practically on top of it to get any warmth—move two inches away and you were freezing again. Whoever's turn it was to buy the ciggies would leave them on top of the heater— twenty Silk Cut for Tracey and twenty Benson & Hedges for Joanne. Then both girls would stand right in front of the fire with their backs to it, each of them with one hand behind her back to warm it and the other with a cigarette in it.

I used to cadge cigarettes from them, and one

morning I came in to find a third packet of ciggies on the heater, for me. I looked at them and felt an enormous sense of acceptance. After that I joined in the ciggie-buying routine, arriving with three packets of cigs when it was my turn and joining the others to smoke in front of the heater.

At lunchtime I used to go to the pub with my friend Susie, and sometimes I went back to her flat for a joint. On 20 December 1986 I went round to her flat as usual. She had loads of Speed. I was regularly taking it on nights out because it sobered me up enough to drink more, but I had hardly ever taken it during the day. I couldn't resist a dab of the bitter-tasting powder, followed by another, and—impatient to feel the effects as soon as possible—yet another. By the time I was ready to go back to work I was buzzing and in overdrive.

The walk to the market normally took seven minutes, but that day I did it in three and sat down in a chair, sweating, with my heart pounding so hard I thought the other girls must surely be able to see it through my jumper. Unable to keep still, I lit one cigarette after another and kept zipping backwards and forwards to the toilet. I was in such a state that I couldn't look anyone in the eye. I was just debating whether to say I was ill and had to go home when Ted walked in. He came over to where I was sitting, knelt down in front of me and said, 'Julie, I'm so sorry, your nan has died.' Norah, who was only sixty-four, had been suffering from cervical cancer for some time and was in a hospice. We all knew that she was going to die, but Ted would have been expecting me to be shocked, upset and tearful—all the normal reactions to a precious grandmother's death. What I did was leap out of

86

my chair, run downstairs to the loo and throw up violently—not because of the news, but because of the drugs that were coursing through my system. I was too high to feel any emotion at all.

Ted, of course, thought my race to the loo was a reaction to Norah's death, and for that I was grateful. I was desperate not to let him know the state I was really in. My chest was still thumping so hard I thought I was going to have a heart attack. I walked back into the room behind the shop and Ted said, 'Sit down, you look terrible.' I did, while attempting to cry—but I couldn't because of the emotionlessness of my drugged condition. Ted mistook my blank white face for shock, and suggested I go home.

In the car on the way home I didn't say a word. When we got in Mum was in the kitchen, in bits. It was Harry's birthday, which only made things harder—Mum was grief-stricken but didn't want him to feel bad. I managed to give her a quick hug and then excused myself and went upstairs to lie on her bed. I couldn't feel anything. I wanted to, and I knew I should, but there was nothing,

I phoned a friend and asked her what I should do. 'My nan's died and I'm buzzing out of my head,' I said.

'Are you allowed out?' she asked.

'Where?'

'It's sixties night at Camden Palace,' she replied.

I decided to go, certain that a couple of drinks would bring me down. My mum, unaware of my state, thought that going out with my friends was just what I needed to get over the shock I was obviously in. So I put on my two-tone puffball skirt, a sleeveless roll-neck top and glitter on my eyes. I

87

tied my hair up and back-combed the ponytail, borrowed some money from Mum and went out and partied all night.

I will always regret that day. I was so close to Norah that her death was the biggest loss I had known in my life. I had seen her almost every day since I was born, and will always remember the love we shared. But on the day she died, because I had taken drugs I felt nothing. It would be a long, long time before I let myself feel the real grief of Norah's death.

I still went to Anna Scher's every week and I still enjoyed being in *Grange Hill*. Acting was something I wanted to go on doing more than anything in the world. When I played a role I became someone else for a while and could forget about being me, leaving everything behind and throwing my whole self into another person's life. I also loved everything that surrounded acting—the team spirit, the fact that I was surrounded by other people all working together for the same end. I became caught up in that and, a bit like when I visited my aunties, I never wanted to leave. Caught up in the togetherness of a production I felt safe, comfortable and more confident than at any other place in my life.

Because acting mattered so much to me I made sure that I was always ready on time and knew exactly what was expected of me. If I had lines to learn (though of course I didn't for *Grange Hill*) I put that ahead of going out and partying. And if I needed to be up early I made sure I got some sleep.

I don't think anyone I worked with suspected I was into drugs. I may have looked tired sometimes—but what teenager doesn't? And although drugs were important to me, acting was even more important, and I wasn't so hooked that I couldn't choose to control what I did and cut back or even give drugs a miss if I had work the next day. I was convinced that no one suspected what I was up to apart from Albert, who knew but wouldn't tell. If Mum worried about what I did when I was out, or why I sometimes behaved a little oddly, then she didn't pursue me about it. So much of her energy was going into the losing battle to stop Albert taking heroin that I think she just hoped and prayed I had learned enough from seeing what happened to him not to go the same way.

Inevitably my *Grange Hill* years had to come to an end—the cast changed frequently as its members outgrew the school, and in 1987, when I was fifteen, I was told that I wouldn't be needed any longer. I felt really sad, because the cast and crew had become like a second family to me. Leaving *Grange Hill* meant I was back to full-time school. By this time I was studying for my GCSEs, or should have been. But I sat through lessons either bored or stoned; what was going on meant very little to me, and school was just something I had to get through to be free at the end of the day. I seldom did my homework and I didn't really think much about a career or how I'd earn a living in due course. It wasn't even that I assumed I'd be an actress—I just didn't think ahead and had no real picture of how the future would be, though I certainly loved acting more than anything else.

After *Grange Hill* several short-term jobs came along. I had a part in an episode of *The Bill* and did ten episodes of a children's TV magic show, which was great fun and earned me membership of the

Magic Circle. The next job couldn't have been more different—I made an information film for a Catholic organization which warned about the dangers of unprotected teenage sex and was intended for use in Irish schools. I played a teenage girl while Joe Wright, who was also at Anna Scher's and who many years later was to direct *Pride and Prejudice*, played my boyfriend. I also appeared in a video for the Red Cross about the dangers of AIDS. The film was considered controversial at the time because AIDS was still connected with the gay community rather than heterosexuals, and the idea that teenagers might be exposing themselves to it had barely been addressed. It got a lot of publicity and I was invited on to the BBC's *Breakfast Time* to talk about it, which I really enjoyed. I made a couple of advertisements, too. One of them was for BT and I was in a family whose members all had ginger hair. My brother was played by Jake Wood, who was at Anna Scher's with me and who in 2006 would join *EastEnders* as Max Branning, father of Bradley and uncle to long-lost Bianca.

In the summer of 1987, only six months after Norah's death, May, my father's mother, died from TB two days before her seventy-sixth birthday. I hadn't been as close to her as I had been to Norah, because Norah was in my life on a daily basis. I always felt that other cousins were closer to Granny because she was their mum's mother. I loved her very much, though. A real earth mother, always kind and caring, she used to go over and see Dad in America and would come back with bags stuffed with gifts for all her grandchildren. At her funeral we buried her next to her beloved husband Albert. She had, for some reason, bought a plot for three graves, and Dad and I always joke about who the third one will be and which one of her kids she meant it for. Luckily they're all still going strong so far.

Dad came over from America and stayed for a couple of weeks after the funeral. After a gap of three years the distance between us felt enormous—far too big to bridge during his brief stay. He went back to the States and it wasn't until 1990, when I was eighteen, that he came back for good and settled in Essex, close to Southend.

After the deaths of both grandmothers and Dad's appearance and disappearance again, all in such a short space of time, I felt a huge sense of loss. And as always with painful feelings I pretended it didn't exist, plastered on a smile and headed out to party. When I took drugs I didn't feel hurt or loss; I felt fabulous, high, excited, full of energy and as though the whole world was my best friend. It was a feeling I wanted to keep all the time, because I knew if I came down I would feel tired, flat, and anxious. The answer was ever more drugs.

Still obsessed by Danny, I felt I loved him and was desperate for him to love me in return. I'm sure a lot of the anxiety and loss I suppressed was poured into my longing for Danny and my dream of being loved by him. I was ready to do anything to keep him and cling to my dream, and not long before my sixteenth birthday I agreed to sleep with him.

A lot of my friends had boyfriends their own age and were having sex for the first time, and I didn't want to be left behind. It was all part of growing up—quite sweet and silly, really, the way we all talked for hours about it, wondering what it would be like. But unlike many of my friends, I found my first experience a complete downer. One night, when we were at a friend's house for a party, Danny and I went into an empty bedroom. In my romantic illusion it was perfect love, but I soon bumped back down to earth when straight afterwards Danny told me he had to go, then just got up and muttered 'See ya' over his shoulder as he went. I sat on the bed wrapped in a duvet, feeling numb with embarrassment and disappointment. Minutes later my friend came in.

'We've done it,' I told her.

'Oh, my God!' she gasped. 'What was it like?'

I wanted to lie and say it had been wonderful, but I couldn't. 'Not very nice,' I admitted, close to tears. 'It was so rough—not loving or special at all. And he was horrible to me. I wish I hadn't done it.'

That night I went home feeling hurt and ashamed and unhappy. I had slept with Danny because I so desperately wanted him to love me, and it hadn't worked. If anything it seemed to make him despise me even more. To me it had been everything, but to him it was nothing. I wished I could turn the clock back, say no to him, keep my clothes on and my dignity intact. But it was too late, and when I got home I lay on my bed and cried.

There was only one thing for it, I decided. I would just have to find a way to make Danny love me. That way everything would be all right and it would take away the horrible feeling that sleeping with him had been a stupid, humiliating mistake.

6

OBSESSING

In the summer of 1988 I left school with a grand total of four GCSEs, in English, English Literature, Drama and Art. It could have been worse, considering how little work I had done, but it was hardly a passport to a glittering career. The one school subject I had always loved was art, so I applied for a foundation course at St Martin's School of Art, but because of my poor GCSEs I was turned down. I felt really useless and had no idea what I was going to do.

That summer I went on my first-ever girls' holiday with my school friends Natalie and Sally. We spent two weeks in a hotel in Tenerife and it should have been wonderful, but instead I spent the whole holiday crying. I missed Danny, even though I hadn't seen much of him lately and he was highly unlikely to have been missing me. But my endless tears probably had more to do with the fact that I had no drugs for the entire time. It was the longest I'd been without drugs of any kind for several years and I hadn't planned to go without—I just couldn't lay my hands on any, and I hadn't realized what hell it would be. I couldn't tell Natalie and Sally because they were from a crowd of friends who weren't into the drug scene. They were more into having a drink, and when I was with them I didn't normally take drugs. Anyway, I blamed my tearful state on pining for Danny, and the girls probably thought I was a real drip for being so down on their hard-earned holiday.

As soon as I got back I rushed round to see Danny, hoping he'd be waiting for me to fall into his arms. He was out, but his brother told me he had a new girlfriend, and that evening I saw for myself that it was true. There was Danny in the pub with a girl draped around him, and he barely noticed me. I went home and this time I genuinely did cry for him. It took me weeks to accept that it was over. I turned up at all the places he usually frequented, hoping to get back together with him. But whenever I saw him he just ignored me. It was humiliating and hurtful, and if I'd had any sense of pride or belief in myself I'd have walked away from him long before. Instead I went home and cried myself to sleep each night, convinced I still loved him.

Broken heart or not, I had to get a job. My art college dream was in tatters so I looked through the local paper, wondering what I could do, and saw an ad for David Bailey Associates. *Wow*, I thought, *could it be David Bailey, photographer superstar?* I rang up and was asked to go for an interview. Excited at the thought of all the models and celebrities I'd be rubbing shoulders with, I made myself look as good as I could and went along.

The office was in the less than glamorous Holloway Road, and I realized the minute I stepped inside and saw people sitting behind desks but no hint of photos—or photographer—that I'd got it wrong. I was gutted, though I'd have been less disappointed if I'd known that one day I would meet *the* David Bailey and be photographed by him. As it was, I thought I might as well stay and talk to the people at the desks. It turned out that the job was cold calling potential customers to sell them life assurance. I explained that as an actress I would need time off if I got an acting job, and they said that was fine. The money was awful, £50 a week plus commission on any sales I made, but I knew I had to start somewhere and so I took the job.

In fact it wasn't that bad. I was one of a number of girls organized in teams who worked our way through the phone book. If someone we called was interested, we'd send round a girl in a smart suit with a company car to try to clinch the deal. Nowadays it probably wouldn't happen, because the girls who went out meeting strangers could so easily have been set up by a psychopath. But in those days we didn't think twice about it. We worked long hours, and those of us on the phones got in the habit of taking caffeine-laden pep pills called Pro-Plus to keep ourselves awake. If we did well we'd be given a bottle of wine at lunchtime—something else that wouldn't happen today. After downing the wine and the pills we'd spend the afternoon completely hyper, and the people on the end of our phones must have thought they'd been called by aliens that sounded like speeded-up cartoon characters.

I stayed in that job for a year or so. I hardly ever earned any commission, despite my best efforts to charm potential customers over the phone. And I never got to meet the David Bailey whose firm it was. He was a bit like Charlie in *Charlie's Angels*— out of sight, but we all felt his presence and knew he was there somewhere.

I was still getting regular acting roles, but

nothing that was really going to get me noticed and they always seemed to involve odd, unflattering costumes. One of the jobs I got around this time was in a television film called *Skulduggery*. Written and directed by Phil Davis, it was the story of three young dropouts and their changing lives. It was a great script, and we spent four or five weeks filming it. I played one of two teenage girls, and my friend Martha the other one, so we had a lot of fun. Most of the boys in the film were friends from acting classes too. I was cast opposite Steve Sweeney, a great actor with a distinctive husky voice. Somehow they made me look really tall and him really small, so it was very comic. I had very long hair and my long, skinny legs stuck out of cowboy boots, which looked terrible. The star was David Thewlis, who would later go on to star opposite Brad Pitt in *Seven Years in Tibet* and as Professor Lupin in the Harry Potter films. David really stood out because he had presence and was such a believable actor. He was also kind and generous, and I was delighted when we acted together a few years later in a film called *Love Story*.

In a second film that year I played another oddball girl. *First and Last* was a BBC production about a retired man who walks from Land's End to John O'Groats, and the people he meets along the way. I was to play a girl he came across who was having an argument with her boyfriend in a car. The star was Irish actor Ray McAnally, who had recently played Daniel Day Lewis's father in *My Left Foot*. We were to shoot my section of the film in Devon and the producer told Mum I'd need a chaperone, so she decided to send Albert, hoping that the responsibility would be good for him and keep him away from trouble. It didn't work—almost as soon as we got there Albert left me with £10 wrapped in a plastic bag and disappeared. I was upset because I'd been looking forward to spending a bit of time with him. But I wasn't bothered about being there on my own—I thought the whole chaperone thing was daft, so rather than tell the producer what had happened I, pretended that Albert was still there and carried on with filming. When Mum found out what had happened she was furious.

Just before filming was completed, in June 1989, tragedy struck. Ray McAnally, who was only sixty-three, died after a heart attack. The decision was taken to reshoot the entire film with a new leading actor, Joss Ackland, and I went down to Devon again, but this time with a chaperone from Anna Scher's.

That year I also appeared in a *Crimestoppers* commercial, a promotional video for the band Jesus Jones and another for Mott the Hoople. They were all fun, but I still didn't have enough work to act full-time. And I'd had enough of sitting in the David Bailey offices cold calling people who didn't want to talk to me and who mostly slammed down the phone. So when the chance came to join Mum and a bunch of other women making fake Chanel perfume, I jumped at it. We all used to meet up in the mornings and travel in a convoy of cars to a remote factory where the stuff was made. It was fun and the money was great—£350 a week cash in hand, which was a fortune then. Sadly, it all came to a dramatic and sudden end when the owner was arrested. I suppose it was predictable, but it was still a bit of a shock, especially as it meant that both Mum and I were instantly out of work.

I looked around for another job and got lucky. Sunbed tanning sessions were the latest thing at that time, and a sunbed shop had opened on the corner of our road. I knew the owner, Jimmy, and he offered me some work: all I had to do was sit and take bookings. My friend Nicole, whom I'd known since primary school, worked there too, and we spent most of our time planning our nights out. On warm days we'd sit on chairs outside the shop and watch the world go by. The shop was always busy—people came in and out all day, so we had lots to gossip about.

I used to go in an hour before work and have a session on the sunbed. I loved it because my pale, freckled skin gradually turned a shade of light golden brown, which I thought was a huge improvement—even though my freckles doubled in number too. In the sun I've always burned, but I could take the sunbed if I was careful. I was totally unaware of the dangers of the sun, or sunbeds—I just knew it was good for the eczema I'd always suffered from. Not that it made me sympathetic to anyone else. One red-haired girl who used to come in had scabs all over her skin: I was convinced she had skin cancer, and banned her. Now I know it was probably just psoriasis, another itchy, uncomfortable skin condition. She was probably just trying to treat it, and I wish I hadn't been so harsh towards her.

The sunbeds in Jimmy's shop were the old kind, with wooden struts on each side and loads of bulbs—really uncomfortable! But despite this I became quite addicted to them and got in as many sessions as I could. My skin became quite brown, and I grew so used to the effect that if it faded a little I thought I looked ill. To my eyes, being brown made me look less wrecked after two days of non-stop bingeing.

Jimmy, my boss, was organizing big warehouse parties which he called Orgasm, and I used to go to them with my mates. I'd also started going to Puscha parties, where everyone wore wigs and dressed up in way-out clothes. The Ecstasy would flow, the music got inside my head and I'd have a ball, dancing for hours on end in jeans and baseball boots. We danced on tables, chairs, radiators and window sills, seas of arms waving in the air, luminous T-shirts and smiley-face badges glowing everywhere. In the summer the parties were sometimes held at the London Astoria and afterwards we'd dance on the parked cars outside and in the fountains at Centre Point, next door. At other times I'd go up to a place called Enter the Dragon in Kensington High Street where I'd party all weekend. After a rave my friends and I would go on somewhere else. Going home just wasn't an option, so we'd go to an after-party gathering or to someone's house. As ever, I was sick many times over the rave weekends, but I loved the high they gave me and wanted them to go on for ever.

It wasn't long before I acquired a new boyfriend. I was still trying to get over Danny when Sean came along and at first I thought they were completely different, because Sean was quieter and much closer to my own age. However, it soon became obvious that Sean was as dangerous and as attractive as Danny had been and I, oblivious to the lessons I should have learned, transferred all my obsessive behaviour to him. Once he'd asked me back to his house a couple of times I was convinced that we were made for one another. Friends warned me that he wasn't really interested, but I refused to see it. So reluctant was he to admit that we were seeing one another that he sometimes told people I was his little sister. That's when he was with me at all. A lot of the time I spent searching clubs and pubs for him, or waiting for him to come home.

Sean worked on a market stall and lived with his brother Gary in Hoxton. I used to go round there all the time looking for him. If Gary was there he'd invite me in and chat to me. But if no one was in when I went round, I'd jump over the fence into the back yard and break into the house. The glass panel in the back door had been smashed and a wood panel nailed over the hole from inside. I used to kick the panel until it came off, the crawl through the door and nail the panel on again when I got inside. Then I'd go up to Sean's room and wait for him—often all night. I did this most Friday nights for months. I had now moved to Anna Scher's Friday evening young professionals group, and I'd sit in the group thinking about Sean and planning to go and see him. Every week I believed it would be different—I was convinced that this time Sean would be in, waiting for me, or would come home and be delighted to find me there. In reality, more often than not he would arrive home at ten o'clock the next morning still drunk and reeking of someone else's perfume, with lipstick marks on his shirt. I was so desperate to get his attention that on one occasion he came home to find me lying motionless on the floor, an empty pill bottle beside me. But my attempts to scare him into loving me failed dismally. Sean glanced down, stepped over me to turn on the TV and snarled, 'Get up.'

I never had the courage to take the pills for real, but I thought about it, sometimes all night as I sat waiting. I felt so lonely and so desperate, and I longed to be brave enough to take them. And Sean's contempt for me only confirmed how worthless I already felt. When he did deign to notice me I was so grateful that I spent money on him, or gave him cash and expensive presents. Most of my earnings had been saved and I persuaded Mum to let me take out enough to buy a Triumph convertible. I was still only sixteen and couldn't even drive yet so she was pretty concerned, but I fobbed her off, telling her that I was going to let Sean drive it until I was old enough to.

After my suicide 'attempt' and Sean's complete indifference to it, I decided I had to break away from him. Nicole suggested a weekend away, so with six other girls and one boy we hired a caravan in Clacton. We had a fantastic weekend, laughing non-stop, and partied at the nightclub there before going back to our caravan. It did me good—I realized I needed to distance myself from Sean and find a life. Nicole was always making new friends and having fun and I felt she was doing what I wished I could do, instead of obsessing over one boy after another.

The funny thing was that, when I pulled back, Sean didn't want to let me go. When I told him it was over he cried and told me he loved me. And at the time I believed him, because he was utterly convincing. Now I think he simply enjoyed controlling me—he was always telling me what I should or shouldn't do. And once I went back to him it wasn't long before he was telling me to fuck off again.

By this time Mum knew about Sean and she was worried. She tried to talk to me about it and she even gave me Robin Norwood's *Women Who Love too Much*. It's a great book and does deal with the kind of obsessive feelings I had, but of course at sixteen I wasn't remotely interested in reading it—I was just annoyed that she thought I had a problem.

I wasn't the only one of her kids giving her grief. Albert was still struggling with his heroin addiction and had finally been persuaded to go to a treatment centre. As part of his treatment I was asked to attend a family therapy session along with Mum, Dad and Harry. The therapist was Beechy Colclough, who later appeared in the press because he treated celebrity clients and was eventually struck off by the British Association for Counselling and Psychotherapy after being accused by some patients of abusing his position as therapist by having sex with them. But at this time Beechy wasn't well known, and what I remember most about that session—we only had one because none of us would go to another—was that he asked me how I felt about Albert's addiction. I was absolutely stumped. No one had ever before asked me how I felt—it just wasn't what our family did. I had no idea what to answer, because I had no idea what I felt. We were more of a 'Cheer up and let's keep going' family than a 'Let's talk about feelings' family.

Albert's stay at the treatment centre didn't make

a lot of difference. It was to be the first of several periods of rehab for him—whenever he came out he went straight back to the drugs. He tried the Twelve Step Programme too. I went with him to one of the meetings, to give him support. At that time I had no idea what the Twelve Steps were about and I thought they were all mad—I got the giggles halfway through and had to leave. Poor Albert must have been mortified, because he was really trying. It was only much later, when I went for myself, that I began to understand the powerful and transformative potential of working those Twelve Steps for yourself.

For Albert, though, the Twelve Step Programme was another failed attempt to get clean. He just wasn't ready to face his addiction, and no programme on earth is gong to work unless you want it to. I feel terribly sad when I think about the course my brother's life has taken. He was good-looking, talented, bright and very creative—indeed he still is. But his addiction has got in the way of anything he might have achieved, which is a tragedy. His battle with drugs has been ongoing and over time the family has distanced itself from him, knowing that there was nothing more we could do for him until he chose to do something for himself. For me it was another loss, because when someone is in the grip of addiction a meaningful relationship becomes almost impossible.

You'd think that seeing what was happening to him would have warned me off. But I was suffering from an addictive personality too—I could never take just a little of anything, be it alcohol or drugs or relationships. I was a binge drinker and a binge drug-taker, and despite the havoc that drugs played in my brother's life and in the lives of many of those around me I still thought taking them was cool and clever. And as for relationships, eventually Sean dumped me in much the same way Danny had. I knew Sean was seeing other girls, but had always turned a blind eye to it until one day I walked into a pub and saw him kissing someone else. I stormed over and demanded to know what he was doing, but he just glanced at me with contempt and said, 'Can't you see I'm busy?'

Humiliated once again, I ran out into the street with tears pouring down my face. I kept telling myself that if only I hadn't gone back to him after the weekend in Clacton this wouldn't have happened. I felt such a fool. Sean had never cared for me, and now I knew it. I promised myself I'd change and find someone different—someone who cared for me and would treat me well. And it wasn't long before a new Mr Right walked—or rather bumped—into my life. I was walking down Bethnal Green Road one day, my head a million miles away, when someone knocked into me so hard that I almost fell over.

'Sorry, love,' he said, in a broad Scottish accent.

I looked up and thought, *Wow, he's gorgeous!* He was tall and dark and was wearing a suit, which in my mind meant he had to be completely different from my past boyfriends. Blushing, I said, 'That's OK. Don't worry about it.'

'Do I know you?' he asked, looking into my eyes.

I knew it was a chat-up line, and I was flattered. That was all he had to say. I was already down the aisle, with him in a kilt and two point four children on the horizon, on our wedding day.

'No, I don't think so,' I giggled.

We got talking and he asked me for a date. We met for a drink two days later and that was it. I was head over heels in love and he was Mr Perfect. His name was Fraser and he was seven years older than me. He worked in insurance—which explained the suit—and lived only a few streets away from me, though we didn't have any of the same friends.

Just like Danny and Sean, Fraser became a magnet for me. We saw each other almost every day, but I still wanted more. Fraser was a drug-user and a heavy drinker, but I didn't see either of those as a problem—after all, I was doing it myself and so were most of the people around me. But it turned out that Fraser was a bit of a gangster, too—he had some very dodgy friends and was always involved in what he called 'business' which took him off to 'meetings' at all kinds of odd times.

I didn't care. Fraser had plenty of money and wore a Cartier watch. I thought I'd stepped up a notch and found the man who'd look after me for the rest of my life. But my Mum got wind of it and banned me from seeing him. Ted knew a bit about his background, and they didn't think he was suitable for me at all. So I started to meet Fraser in secret, which made it all the more exciting. We'd get together in clubs and hotels and I thought it was all very romantic—so romantic that I ignored the indications that Fraser had a very dark side to him. When he began standing me up, I told myself he'd had to work late. And when he snapped viciously at me one night, I told myself he was stressed.

I was back in the same cycle, but I couldn't admit it. Fraser loved women and they loved him. He was often surrounded by women at clubs, and he'd ignore me for most of the evening and then be horrible to me when we left. Time after time I was left nursing a drink in a pub because he'd gone off to see to some 'business', or just hadn't turned up in the first place. I should have seen the signs and walked away, but I was incapable of doing that. Even though he often treated me like dirt, I clung on to the memory of how he'd been in the first few weeks, when he was sexy and funny and behaved as though he thought I was too. I was sure that that was the 'real' Fraser and that the surly drunk with the sharp tongue was just a temporary blip.

What it is to be in denial! You can convince yourself of anything—and I did, for almost a year, until on my eighteenth birthday the blinkers finally fell away. It was May 1990 and I was excited about becoming an official adult at last. But the story of my birthday is one of the saddest stories of my life and sums up just how far from being a real adult I was. Balanced, wise, clear-headed and self-respecting? I was a million miles from achieving any of those qualities. Lost, foolish, deaf to advice and with zero self-esteem would be closer to the truth.

I had dreamed of spending the day with Fraser, going shopping, having a meal out and making it a really special day. But it was just that—a dream. We did spend part of the day together. We went to Covent Garden, to Fraser's favourite shop, American Classics. On the wall inside was a poster of two good-looking boys. One of them was Nick Love, who would later become my first husband. But I didn't know Nick then, and although I thought he looked cute my eyes were fixed on Fraser. Desperate to buy his love, I splashed out on jeans and a gorgeous pair of boots for him. Needless to say, he bought me nothing. But I didn't mind—I'd bought myself a new dress for the date I believed we were going on in the evening. Then Fraser told me that he was going out to a club with some mates instead. It was a blow, but I found a solution. I would go home and get ready, as planned, then surprise him at the club.

When I got home from the shopping trip I slipped into the house, planning to change quickly and do my hair and make-up before going to meet Fraser. Then Mum asked me to come into the garden for a moment. There, waiting for me with big grins on their faces, were my brothers, Dad—who had just moved back from the States—aunties, cousins, schoolfriends and other pals. It was a surprise party. Shocked, I turned to look at Mum who was smiling delightedly, waiting for me to look pleased. I didn't. I was furious. I hadn't wanted a party at home—I wanted to be with Fraser. But I couldn't say anything—my family didn't know I was still seeing him, and even so wouldn't have invited him as they were convinced he was bad news.

A glass of champagne was put into my hand as everyone gathered round to wish me happy birthday. I was touched that they'd all taken so much trouble, and in a way I wanted to stay and enjoy being princess for the evening. But I couldn't. Not even the sight of Richie, Harry's friend and my secret crush since the age of eleven, was enough to keep me there.

I drank my champagne, hastily cut my cake, then turned round and went back into the house. As I put my new dress on I was crying, because I knew that what I was doing was crazy and awful and I was hurting almost everyone I cared about. But I couldn't stop myself. On the way out I told Mum I was sorry, but I couldn't stay. She didn't even bother to ask where I was going. I tried to ignore the expression on her face, but it was hard to forget just how mortified she looked. Still, I was going to see Fraser and that's what I really wanted. It was my birthday, after all, and my choice. I rushed round to his house, hoping to catch him there and go to the club with him, but he had already gone. Never mind—I knew where they were meeting, so I got on the Tube and raced down there.

When I got to the club Fraser was sitting there with his mates and a couple of girls. I went over to them, nervous but smiling and doing my best to look gorgeous in my new outfit. Fraser turned, looked at me coldly and said, 'Go away.'

'What?' I asked him. I thought I must have misheard.

'Go away,' he repeated.

'What do you mean?' I said, my face scarlet with embarrassment.

Fraser got up, grabbed my arm and practically dragged me out of the place. Then he punched me in the face. 'That's what I mean,' he said. He turned and went back inside, leaving me clutching my smarting, throbbing face and feeling so sick with fury and shame that I wanted to lie down and die. Despite many awful scenes in the past, no one had ever hit me before. Crying so much that I could hardly walk, I practically crawled back on to the Tube. I couldn't go home—I knew my birthday party would still be going on without me, and I was too humiliated and distraught to join in. So I walked around for a couple of hours in a daze, then

108

slipped into the house when it was all over and crept into bed.

When I woke up the next morning I knew I had to end it. He didn't want me, he didn't even like me, and I had sunk to pitiful depths trying to make him care. I had to find the courage to break away. That day I pretended I had slipped and banged my face on a door in a pub. I don't know whether anyone believed me, but I was grateful that they pretended to. Then I started to hope that Fraser would get in touch to apologize. How could he fail to, when he had been so awful to me? He'd say sorry, and we'd make up and put it behind us, wouldn't we?

But quickly I looked at my bruised and swollen face in the mirror. *He did that to you*, I told myself, *and you're thinking that it will all be OK?* I realized that I was heading for the kind of relationship where I'd be a battered wife, cowed and humiliated by a brutal man. The thought really frightened me. Did I think that was all I deserved? I knew my friends were worried about me. Most of my girlfriends were settling into relationships with nice men, and here I was searching out men who didn't give a toss about me and who took pleasure in humiliating me. I had to stop.

I made myself a promise that I would never let myself be treated so badly again. And when Fraser rang me—not even mentioning the assault—I told him to get lost. After I put down the phone I was shaking, but I'd done it, and for the first time in ages I felt proud of myself.

7

PREGNANT

What had happened with Fraser shook me badly. I had got into a damaging and destructive relationship, and it frightened me to realize how pathetic and desperate my behaviour had been. I didn't want to risk anything like that again and for the next few weeks I stayed away from men, afraid to trust my own judgement.

It was ironic that I was wary of men but not of drugs, which were the real source of my problems. Despite the fright I'd had, it didn't occur to me that the huge quantities I was taking might have impaired my judgement or disconnected me from myself to the extent that I allowed appalling things to happen to me. The effect of the drugs was so pervasive that effectively I was never fully present in my own life. I was like a person watching a film about someone else, unable to intervene or to change the course of events. I couldn't make a clear decision or discriminate between good and bad. And I didn't even know it. I thought I was fine—apart from having dodgy taste in men.

When my friend Mandy suggested we go on holiday to Ibiza I jumped at the chance. I wanted to get away from home for a while, and from things that reminded me what a fool I'd made of myself with a man who despised me. But though that holiday might have been a break from home and routine, it wasn't a break from drugs. We lay on the beach all day and partied all night: drugs were freely available and we took full advantage. We went out each night and got back to our hostel at ten or eleven the next morning, when we loaded our bags and towels on to our hired scooter and set off for the beach. I hated driving the scooter so I'd usually sat on the pillion, clinging on to Mandy with one arm and the lilo with the other. Then we slept on the beach all day. It was a crazy way to behave, but I thought it was great. I was young, free and single—I could do anything I wanted.

When we got back, my friends and I started going to a new pub round the corner from where I lived. I was glad of the change, because I didn't want to be anywhere that Fraser might appear. And it was in the new pub that I met Eddie. He was good-looking, attractive, kind and fun, and best of all he wanted me—for the first time in my life someone else was doing the chasing. He asked a friend of mine, 'Who's that girl?' and I was thrilled when I heard about it. We got talking and I liked him immediately. It was a relief to fancy someone who seemed so normal and nice, and when Eddie asked me out I said yes.

At first I was afraid that soon enough I'd find that the real Eddie was just another bad guy who'd hurt me and mess me around. I'd been so dreadfully wrong in the past—had I really managed to pick someone different this time? It seemed that for once I really had. I saw Eddie for about six months, and it was a taste of what life should be like for a girl of eighteen. Unlike most of my previous boyfriends he was only a couple of years older than me, and we had a nice time doing normal things: going to the pub, to the cinema and to each other's homes. Eddie cared for me and wanted to be with me; he made me feel special, and if I'd had any sense I'd have stayed with him. But after only a few months I bumped into Fraser again. After that it seemed as if everywhere I went I came across him. And every time I saw him he did his best to convince me that he'd changed, that he loved me and that I should be with him and not with 'that boring jerk', as he called Eddie. He sent me records, like Sinead O'Connor's 'Nothing Compares to You' and Phil Collins's 'You Can Run and You Can Hide'. He promised me he'd learned his lesson and, although I'm embarrassed to admit it, I fell for it. I dropped Eddie, who couldn't understand why I was ending something so good, and went back to Fraser.

Neither of us had changed at all, of course. He was still a monster and I was still so brainwashed by drugs that I couldn't see it. For a week he was nice to me, and I had the illusion that all would be well. But then things started to go downhill—fast. Within days I realized that Fraser's drinking was spiralling out of control, and when he drank he got violent. After our second week back together he got into a fight with another guy outside a club and then threatened to hit me again. Frightened and shocked, I couldn't believe I'd been stupid enough to go back to him or to think he might have changed.

I knew I had to break away once more, but how? Fraser had already proved that he wasn't going to let me go. I was certain that even if I found the courage to leave him a second time he'd follow me and try to persuade me to go back to him. And if that failed, I didn't doubt that he might turn very nasty. I decided the only way was to get as far away as possible. Some friends were planning a backpacking holiday to Thailand over Christmas and the New Year and I decided to join them. We planned to be away for two months, and I was excited because apart from a few package holidays I hadn't really done any travelling. This was going to be a real adventure.

I was grateful that Mum had always saved the money I earned from acting. I was still getting regular jobs such as one-off appearances in TV series like *The Bill* or in advertisements, though nothing big had come along for a while. But I had enough put by to cover the trip. There was only one thing I dreaded: flying. I decided the only way to get through it was to sedate myself and then consume vast quantities of chocolate. So before we took off on our cheapie flight to Bangkok via Moscow I took a couple of Valium, then bought a huge box of Quality Street to take on to the plane and ate the lot.

A few of our friends had already been to Thailand and they'd talked about the amazing beach parties, the raves and, of course, the cheap drugs. So we arrived in Bangkok expecting it to be brilliant, but in fact I found it a little scary. With my colouring I really stood out, and everywhere I went women would come up and touch my hair. I got another shock when I went for a massage—I had no idea that massage and sex are virtually synonymous in Thailand. I was very prudish about sex; where I came from you never mentioned it because it was considered a disgusting subject, and if you talked about it openly you were a slag. I had only ever slept with a boyfriend when I felt I was really in love, so I nearly fell off the massage table when the masseuse casually asked if I wanted sex with my massage. Needless to say, I bolted out of there as fast as I could.

I saw the sad side of the sex industry there, too. I met one little girl of eleven who told me she was a prostitute. She was very matter-of-fact about it— her mother and aunts were prostitutes too, all of them, like so many women in Thailand, trying to earn enough money to survive and to help their desperately poor families.

Meanwhile I was beside myself with excitement when I realized that in Bangkok you could get brilliant fakes of designer gear and jewellery for pennies rather than pounds. These were the days before fakes were everywhere, so we bought lovely bags and all kinds of goodies to show off back home.

Then we headed for the coastal resort of Pattaya, where we planned to spend Christmas. I didn't really like Pattaya, which wasn't the Thailand I had imagined. I wanted the full moon and beach parties, but Pattaya was just a strip of endless bars and clubs. There were lots of public kick-boxing rings in which opponents would fight and sometimes literally kick each other's heads in. On Christmas Eve I was standing in the crowd, watching one of these fights, when I turned round to discover that my friends had disappeared. They were in fact in a bar close by, and had thought I was with them. But at the time I had no idea where they were, so I walked up and down trying to find them. A few lads were passing, and I asked if they had seen the girls I was with. As I did so, two of them started fighting. I wasn't sure if the fight was real or a game, but the next moment one of them swung round and punched me in the face. The pain was searing, but instead of helping me the boys panicked and ran off.

I was left standing in the street, scared and alone, with a split, bleeding lip and no idea what to do. *How did this happen to me?* I thought. *I've come to the other side of the world to escape a violent guy, and I manage to get myself punched in the face!* Feeling terribly sorry for myself I went into the nearest bar and sat there alone, nursing a coconut cocktail and a very swollen, sore, lip. I was about to leave when the floorshow began. Dolled up in sparkly outfits, two transvestites sang in falsetto voices as they danced and writhed. The next minute one of them came across and sang, 'You can ling my bell', leaning seductively right over me while totally ignoring the state of my face. I had to laugh.

After a while I left and managed to find a taxi, which took me back to the tiny, grim hotel where the others were waiting for me. There followed a night journey crammed in a boat with so many others that it was barely possible to breathe and I was convinced we'd capsize at any moment, but finally we arrived at the beautiful resort of Koh Samui. From there we went to Koh Pang Yang, where we rented little huts on the beach. People were camped out all along it: old hippies who'd been there for years, new hippies, honeymooners and backpackers, all ready to party.

One evening someone told us about a restaurant that sold great omelette and chips. As there weren't many places I could eat, since I hated anything spicy and refused the local food, I jumped at the chance. That night the menu was indeed offering 'magic mushroom omelette and chips'. We knew magic mushrooms were supposed to have hallucinatory effects but we'd never tried them, and so, intrigued, we ordered one each. They were delicious, but didn't seem to have any odd effects—until we got halfway home when we suddenly started to trip like never before. That night I joined some backpackers in their hut, where I swung in their hammocks and laughed for the next six hours. In fact I laughed so much I made myself sick. Hardly the magic experience I'd hoped for.

We spent the last few weeks chilling on the beach, with no sense of time and nothing particular to do. Being so far away from home was good for me and gave me a chance to do some serious thinking. *Why did I always head straight for guys who treated me like dirt?* I wondered. *Was I up to finding and sticking with a good man? Or was there a part of me that just wouldn't believe I deserved anything good?* I spent a lot of time going over it in my head, and promising myself I'd make a fresh start.

After travelling for over two months our money had run out and it was time to head home. By this time I was missing my family and friends badly, and it was wonderful to see them all and catch up on what had happened while I was away. I had been out of a relationship for the whole time I was away and it had given me some useful mental space. While I was still taking drugs, and therefore often still very dissociated from myself and my real feelings, I could see clearly enough to know that I never wanted to get involved with another Fraser. *This time*, I told myself, *it really will be different.*

The contrast between Thailand's golden beaches and Bethnal Green in February was hard to adjust to. But I'd spent all my money and needed to work to earn some more, so a week or two after my return I got a job on a stall in East Street market selling tracksuits for a man called Mick, who was a friend of Mum's partner Ted. I had to get up at five in the morning, meet the boys I worked with in a café for breakfast and then help them set up the stall. At that time in the morning it was freezing cold, dark and a real struggle to get going.

One night I was in the pub with some friends when I ran across a guy I'd known for a few years. We'd always liked one another, but in the past either he'd been with someone else or I had. This time we were both free, and we got talking and seemed to click. After the break from relationships I was ready to be swept off my feet, and he obliged: for the next few months we had a passionate romance. He wasn't as sweet as Eddie, but he wasn't a Fraser either, and I thought I'd done pretty well in choosing him. I could see he wasn't the type to settle down, but it didn't seem to matter—we were having fun, in any case and I wasn't ready to settle down myself.

By late June, when we'd been together four months, I was beginning to feel really ill in the mornings. I couldn't understand it, because I didn't go wild on the nights when I knew I was working the next day—with a five o'clock start I couldn't handle it. But I still felt so ill that I'd sit in the café groaning, while the guys laughed at me and told me I couldn't hack it.

One day I was at home with Mum when I started to feel really sick, worse than anything I'd felt before. I was so ill I wanted to die, and Mum got really worried. When I wasn't better by the next day she insisted on taking me to hospital. After a thorough examination the doctor came in with some shocking news. I wasn't ill after all. I was pregnant.

I was horrified—and yet at the same time excited. Pregnancy had been the last thought on my mind because I was on the Pill. But then again, because of all the drink and drugs I had been erratic about taking it, so perhaps I shouldn't have been as stunned as I was.

After the news had sunk in I wondered what on earth I was going to do. The baby's father and I were nowhere near ready to move in together, let alone become parents. But on the other hand I loved children, and I couldn't help feeling that this was the beginning of something miraculous.

There was never really any question about keeping the baby—I couldn't possibly have done anything else. Mum was so relieved that I wasn't ill that she immediately told me not to worry and that she'd support and help me. I was glad she was so positive about it, but I was far less sure that the baby's father would feel the same way. He'd gone on holiday to Greece with some mates, but I managed to ring him and break the news. He wasn't too thrilled to hear, but we agreed to talk when he got back. We did, and decided to make a go of the relationship for the baby's sake. But I'm not sure that either of us felt very confident about it lasting. After all, he wasn't in a position to support me and our baby, or find us a home. Still, we thought we'd give it our best shot.

I stopped drinking and taking drugs the minute I knew I was pregnant. I knew I had to do so for the baby, and that I might find things really tough, but it was made much easier for me by the fact that I felt so sick I couldn't have faced drink or drugs anyway. I was ill throughout the whole nine months, and became so dehydrated from vomiting that I was regularly going into hospital to be hooked up to a drip to try to get some fluid into me. Unsurprisingly I had to give up my job on the stall, which in the circumstances was just too much.

The whole family rallied round wonderfully. Harry was very protective and managed to get me a housing association flat in the same block as himself. He was a fantastic brother: although he was the same age as my baby's father, to me he seemed so much older because he had got his life together. I moved into the flat when I was six months pregnant. Everyone came over to help with the decorating and I tried to make it into a proper home for the baby. The place was tiny—just one small bedroom, a living room, kitchen and bathroom—but it was all I needed. Soon afterwards my boyfriend moved in too, but we weren't getting on brilliantly and he was almost always out.

Being pregnant forced me to take things a lot more seriously. I was determined to love and protect this baby, so I tried really hard to do all the right things, turning up to hospital appointments and making sure I got enough sleep. I tried to eat well, but eating often made me sick and it was hard to keep any food down.

For the first time my old schoolfriend Nicole seemed to be having a serious relationship with a guy. Jason was lovely, and the two of them did everything they could to help me. They bought presents for the baby and took me out for meals—

which, of course, more often than not I couldn't keep down. But I was so grateful for their kindness and support. They often came round just to spend an evening with me watching movies, which can't have been very exciting for them.

Dad and Marcelle had been back from America for a couple of years by this time and had settled in Essex, near Southend. I went to see them every now and then and it was always good to catch up with him, but, sadly, after six years apart we couldn't really forge the kind of father–daughter relationship I would have liked. He was always lovely to me and offered to help in any way he could, but I seldom asked him for anything. However, while my relationship with Dad was fairly distant, with my cousins—his sisters' children—it was quite the opposite. They helped me a lot at this time, and we all became very close.

It was a strange time for me, preparing for my new life yet not knowing what to expect, still barely more than a child myself and yet about to bring a child into the world. Emotionally I was still very young and unprepared. I spent the last few weeks of my pregnancy worrying whether my baby would be safe. I was still feeling sick most of the time, and often I was actually being sick too. I could eat very little and was always afraid that I might miscarry or that all the vomiting might have damaged the baby. As I worried about things, day after day, I came to realize how much I loved this child. I realized that it didn't matter what else happened as long as my baby was all right.

8

CHARLEY—AND *EASTENDERS*

My baby was due on 4 February 1992, but the day came and went with no sign of me going into labour. A few days later I was round at my mum's when pains started.

'This is it,' I told her.

'No, it isn't,' Mum said. 'You look much too cheerful.'

Mum knew I was in labour, but she also knew it would probably be hours before the real pain started, so she decided to distract me and keep me busy. She was going over to Ted's daughter Tracey's flower shop in Leytonstone to collect some things she'd left there, and took me with her. We parked the car and walked a short distance to the shop, where Mum gave me a mop and bucket to carry back to the car while she took some other things. As I walked along I kept having to stop, as waves of pain shot through my back and my stomach. Nevertheless we kept laughing at the thought of what we must have looked like, me with my massive bump and my mop and bucket, and Mum beside me with her shopping bags rubbing my back.

When we got home she made something to eat, though I wasn't able to get much down, and then we went to my flat to get the things I would need for hospital. Mum phoned them, but they told her it was too soon and she shouldn't bring me in yet. So I walked in circles round the room, stopping every few minutes as the pain got worse.

Eventually I told Mum I was sure I really needed to go in now. It was almost midnight when we arrived at Homerton Hospital, a few minutes from home. As soon as I walked through the doors the pain really kicked in and I doubled over. Mum raced to get a wheelchair and I was taken straight to the labour ward. Although I was shocked by the intensity of the pain I didn't want an epidural, because I'd heard of someone dying after having one. So they gave me Pethidine, which made me feel completely out of it. I sat up in bed and shouted, 'Hello, everyone!', then started singing an advertising jingle that was on the TV at the time: 'Mrs Moore, don't pay any more.' Goodness knows what the other patients and the nurse thought as Mum tried to shush me and calm me down.

I was happy on the Pethidine, which felt just like Ecstasy. The pain had gone and I wanted some more, but the nurses refused to give me any as I'd already had the safe limit. Instead I was given gas and air, through a mask that I kept so tightly clamped to my face that I almost knocked myself out with it. I had always thought I would scream my head off in labour, but most of the time I was silent, crippled with fear and too scared to breathe, let alone scream. I kept my eyes focused on the clock, ticking loudly in front of me on the wall, but I felt as though time had somehow slowed down as the hands never seemed to move. They must have moved, though, because I was actually in labour for twelve hours. And eventually, after one enormous scream, my baby was born.

I was still so out of it on the Pethidine I'd had earlier that when I set eyes on my baby I shouted,

'Oh, my God! I've given birth to a gremlin.' I'd never seen a newborn baby and had no idea they were covered in so much blood and gunk. 'No, love, it's a lovely little boy. Congratulations,' the midwife said. The nurses were reluctant to hand him to me as I was so spaced out, but Mum was telling them, 'Give her the baby,' because she wanted me to bond with him. At this point I ran into the bathroom, sat on an orange plastic chair, grabbed the shower head and poured water over myself. I must have looked totally mad—I was so out of it I had no idea what I was doing. Mum and the midwife had to come and get me, dry me off and put me back into bed.

I was handed my son and Mum later described how my face changed as I looked into his eyes and love overwhelmed me. He was simply gorgeous, with big blue eyes looking up at me from his wrinkled little pink face, and little tufts of blond hair sticking up on his head. I named him Charley, a name I loved and which suited him. His father had arrived in time for the birth and, despite all his uncertainty about family life, was thrilled to have a son.

I wasn't in hospital for long. Within a day or so we were discharged and went back to the flat, where I had a Moses basket, baby-gros and piles of nappies waiting. All our family and friends came to see Charley. I loved having a baby, but found the reality of coping really hard. I was too young and it was such a shock suddenly to be a mum. I had absolutely no idea how to feed, change or look after a baby, and his father certainly didn't. Although he was proud of Charley we weren't getting on and he wasn't into hands-on baby care, so he continued to disappear most of the time. Thankfully, Mum was fantastic and visited me every day for the first few weeks, showing me how to get into a routine.

It was tough, at nineteen, living in a tiny rented flat on benefits of £70 a week—my savings were long gone—with a baby to look after, no work and a very shaky arrangement with an on/off partner. The relationship came to an end when Charley was a few months old and we agreed to separate, after which I was officially a single parent—though I'd felt like one most of the time anyway. We tried to keep things amicable but were unable to agree over my ex-boyfriend's access to Charley, which led to a legal dispute that took some time to resolve.

Despite being on my own, I wasn't unhappy. In fact in some ways it was a relief to be out of the relationship instead of wondering whether it could be made to work or not. Things were peaceful in the flat with just Charley and me, and I decided I didn't want another man in my life for a while. Most days I went round to Mum's, and she often gave me a lifeline by taking Charley so that I could see friends and go out. She'd take him to work in the factory with her, putting his little car seat beside the machine where she was working. And there he'd nod off, soothed by the hum of the sewing machines. Mum and Ted were fantastic to me during those early years. They made it possible for me to have a social life and to work when opportunities came along—I'm so grateful to them.

To be honest, I left Charley with my mum more often than I should have. I loved him with all my heart, but I found it hard being a parent and being with him all the time. Before I had a baby I'd been used to going out almost every night, and although I got used to nights in with him I still needed to see my friends. The trouble was, seeing my friends meant drinking and taking drugs again. Although I'd managed without drugs during my pregnancy and for a few weeks after the birth, as the sickness wore off I discovered I still craved them and couldn't wait to get high again. I didn't see Charley's birth as an opportunity to give up permanently, because I didn't think I had a problem.

So while Mum and Ted looked after my son, I went off partying and getting off my head on anything I could get my hands on. The difference was that now I felt terribly guilty. I knew what I was doing wasn't fair to Mum or to Charley. But, guilty or not, I carried on. Mum still seemed to have no idea what I was up to, and I was convinced she just wanted me to be a normal young girl and spend time with my friends. She certainly didn't begrudge me staying over at a friend's house after a party, even though I did it time after time. But later I would discover that I was blissfully naïve in thinking that Mum didn't have any suspicions. She did fear that I was into drugs, but not knowing for sure, and feeling helpless after her losing battle to help Albert, she chose to turn a blind eye and hope that if I was taking drugs I wouldn't do anything too foolish.

My partying would always end the same way. I'd wake up the next morning and give anything to be at home with Charley, instead of retching over a loo in some freezing cold bathroom and having to take another sip of brandy to ease the nausea. That was my sad reality. Part of the problem was that

125

none of my friends had a baby, so I had no one to share my feelings with or who understood the different pulls on my life. While I loved my baby with all my heart, I found living with him very hard. The reality of being a single mother was hours spent alone in a tiny flat with only a baby for company, and it made me restless and edgy. I wasn't good at being alone because I wasn't comfortable enough with myself, and I craved escape into the chemical high which I knew would blot out anything uncomfortable.

So I avoided being alone, and soon the parties were taking over and I was leaving Charley with Mum for most of each weekend. My friends and I had started going over to Loughton in Essex, where there was a bar there that we liked. We used to drink there on Friday nights, then on Saturdays we'd go to Legends nightclub, our favourite at that time, after which I'd invite everyone back to my flat to party for the rest of the night. Then on Sundays we'd go to the Epping Forest Country Club. Party weekends in fact often lasted from Friday to Tuesday. Mum tried hard to get me to spend more time with Charley, but I'd beg her to take him and let me go out and, despite her concerns, she usually gave in.

I had an old Renault and used to drive around in it even when I was full of drugs and alcohol, taking so many appalling risks it's a wonder I'm still alive. Once a tyre blew as I was driving along but I just kept going, and when I got home I found it was frayed like a bit of old rag. I thought the whole thing was hilarious and hung the object on the wall in my flat. I had no fear at all, and no idea of the danger I was putting myself in—on the contrary, I thought I was a fantastic driver.

In May 1993 I turned twenty-one. That birthday was a little better than my eighteenth, but not a lot. I had a party in the bar in Loughton with both my brothers and lots of my friends including Richie, Harry's mate. When I was eleven and he was nineteen the age gap had seemed so big: he'd been an adult while I was still a child, and I'd looked up to him. But now we were both adults in our twenties the difference had shrunk, and I counted him as a friend of mine as well as of Harry's. I still had a little flutter in my stomach every time I saw him, but I was sure he wasn't interested in me—after all, he'd only ever treated me as a mate—and so I settled for being his friend.

I was having a great time at my party, off my head on drugs as always and convinced I was loving it, when things started to go badly wrong. A fight broke out among several of the boys, all of them high on drugs, and things rapidly escalated. Soon the girls were screaming as the boys laid into one another viciously. It was typical of the kind of sordid scene that could break out at any time in our drug-dominated world, and it only ended when the bar manager ordered us all to leave and threatened to call the police. It was dreadful, but I just thought it was funny. After we'd left we wandered around for a while and then a few of us went to a hotel, where we carried on drinking. We tried to keep the party going, but in truth it was over before it began. Another sad, wasted birthday.

The next day I went to my mum's, still wearing the same outfit. I wasn't sure if I was acting normally or not, because I'd had so many drugs the night before, but I thought Mum would assume I'd had lots to drink and no sleep and put my babbling, incoherent chatter down to that. She wasn't a fool, though, and she knew someone on drugs when she saw her. I didn't realize this because, hard as it must have been for Mum, she said nothing. She was well aware that I wouldn't listen, and that eventually I would have to decide for myself whether to do something about the situation.

Like most addicts, I was totally self-absorbed and unable to see beyond the end of my nose. Oblivious to Mum's worry and distress, I told myself she didn't know and ignored the very obvious anxiety on her face. I regret that now, very much. And I'm grateful that she was always there for me. I loved to sit in her kitchen after an all-night session, feeling safe and protected as I had when I was a little girl. I'd tell her stories from the night before—edited, of course—and feel really close to her.

Inevitably I did no acting work the year I had Charley and for a while afterwards. But my hopes were as strong as ever and I still went to Anna Scher's young professionals group once a week and dreamed of getting that big break. Gradually I began going for parts again and in 1993, when Charley was one, I began to get busy. I appeared in another episode of *The Bill*, playing a battered wife. Charley was in it too, as my baby; he slept the whole way through, not fazed a bit by the lights, cameras and voices. I was playing alongside an actor called Eddie Marsden, who lived opposite me in Bethnal Green and went on to star in lots of films including Martin Scorsese's *Gangs of New York*.

Around that time I was also in an episode of a

drama about a limousine company called *Full Stretch*—playing a heroin addict again—and an episode of the cult comedy programme *Drop the Dead Donkey*, a favourite of mine. In that one I was a girl living in a squat, acting alongside a shy, modest, sweet actor called Daniel Craig. He was very talented, but I never in a million years imagined he would one day be James Bond! Those were the days when we still associated Bond with suave, old-school actors like Sean Connery and Roger Moore. Daniel didn't have a hint of the suave about him. He did have amazing eyes, though—really deep, sexy, come-to-bed eyes. So perhaps there was a touch of Bond about him after all—and as it turned out he was brilliant in the part.

One day Anna Scher announced that casting director Jane Deitch and writer-director Tony McHale from *EastEnders* were coming to visit. They were looking for a girl of sixteen or under who would be part of a new family that Tony was creating for the show. I wasn't on the list of people for them to see, because I was too old. As Tony and Jane watched the people on the list do their stuff, I was mucking around at the side of the class with my friend Melissa and taking no notice of them. Anna kept telling us to shush and apologizing to Tony and Jane, but I was in a silly mood and couldn't stop giggling. Towards the end of the class Tony said he'd like to see me do something. Anna, who'd been irritated with me all through the class, immediately smiled and said, 'Ah, Patsy, one of our best actresses.' She asked me to improvise a monologue based on a line she gave me, which was 'I can't believe you just said that.' I hadn't expected to be performing and was taken by surprise, but I did my best.

Tony and Jane thanked me and left, and I didn't think a lot about it after I went home. I was sure I hadn't done that well and must be last in the running for the part, thinking they probably just wanted someone to contrast with the girls they'd been looking at. But the next day Anna rang to say they wanted me to go to Elstree for an audition. I was wild with excitement. I loved *EastEnders* by this time and never missed an episode, especially as I knew a few of the people in it. Gilly Taylforth I knew from Anna's and my old mate Sid Owen had been in the cast for the past five years, playing none-too-bright mechanic Ricky Butcher. I loved watching him and used to think, *If only I could be in this show—I know I could be really good.* Could I really be about to get a part alongside him? I could hardly believe it, and tried not to let my hopes get too high. And there was a dilemma, too. Should I tell them I was a single mum with a year-old son? Would they still be happy to give me the part, or would they worry that I might be unreliable? I decided to play it safe and not say anything.

As I drove to Elstree in my battered maroon Renault I couldn't help dreaming of buying a new green Ford Fiesta with four doors. My Renault only had two, and getting Charley's car seat in and out was a nightmare. A four-door model would make life so much easier, and if I got a part in the show for a few months I just might be able to buy one. Second-hand, of course. A new car was beyond my wildest dreams.

When I arrived I was shown in to see Tony McHale and a couple of producers. I didn't know it

Reading the News at Ten, aged about four.
Thanks for the perfectly straight parting,
Mum!

My parents and
their friends at a
bit of a boozy do
My dad is standi
on the left, my
mum is the wom
who looks just
like me!

The day of my christening, with
my beloved grandparents.

This is me and my oth
nan, who I was also clo
to. Family has always
been a big deal in the
East End.

A school photo, taken when I was about 12. By this point I'd virtually dropped out.

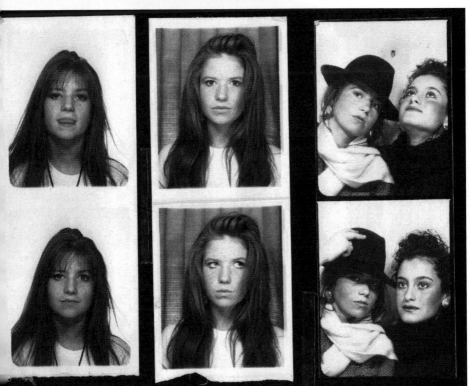

Being a teenager . . . I loved dressing up and having a laugh.

Having a
laugh had
a habit of
getting out
of hand.
Even at
13, I never
knew
when to
stop.

Me and Farvy. This was taken on my eighteenth
birthday and my eyes are still red from crying.

I was 19 when I had Charlie. I adored him but I felt (and looked!) so young.

Mum gave me so much help. I couldn't have done it without her.

Charlie in one hand, drink in another.
I never went off the rails when I was
looking after him but it was a different
story when I wasn't.

I was a huge party girl. This was taken in Ibiza, the morning after the night before.

I never ever knew when to stop. I would have said I wa just having fun but actually I was living a lie.

EastEnders was my big break and I absolutely loved it.
Bianca was just a brilliant character to play.

Me and
Martine, on
the set in the
Queen Vic.
She was a
really good
friend to me.

Me and Robbie Williams having a giggle in my dressing room. You never knew who you might bump into hanging out round the studios.

Crashed out in my dressing room. I didn't let drugs get i the way of my job but sometimes I was too exhausted t stay awake between scenes.

Ricky and Bianca's wedding was a huge TV moment. This is me and Sid in front of the camera . . .

. and the mayhem behind it! The police had to keep the public away from the filming.

Me, Lucy and Angela at the Phoenix Festival in 1997. Ju[st] hours later I suffered a breakdown.

Me and Charlotte, when we were still drinking buddies rather than business partners.

The wild times were getting out of control but life went on, on the surface. Meeting the Queen was a huge thrill.

With Martin Kemp, winning an *Elle* Style Award. I hadn't thought for a moment I would win, so I was over the moon!

Richard is the love of my life. When we got together I finally realised what love was all about.

Our wedding day, with Charley and Fenton. I felt like the happies woman in the world.

The Twelve Step Programme saved my life and enabled me to be reconciled with Mum. It felt so good.

almer-Cutler turned out nice again...

I absolutely love being a businesswoman. Me and Charlotte had a real laugh doing these photos.

On the up . . .
So many
brilliant things
have happened
to me since I
went into
recovery. From
dancing my
socks off . . .

. . . to getting
accolades for roles in
*He Knew He was
Right* . . .

. . . to doing my bit for Mind, who used this photo in one of their campaigns to raise awareness of mental health issues . . .

. . . to exploring my new-found spiritual side through painting, which I love!

But the single most important thing in my life these days
my family. This is me on holiday with Emilia, our nanny
Arte, Richard, Charley and Fenton. I love you all!

at the time, but Tony and Jane had pretended to the producers that I was sixteen in order to get them to see me. If they'd known my real age they'd have refused, because they were adamant they wanted a young girl for the part. The three of them chatted to me for a while, got me to tell them a bit about myself, and then asked me to read some of the script. It was the part of Bianca Jackson, a mouthy, opinionated, hot-headed sixteen-year-old who was about to arrive in the Square with the rest of her family.

I left with no idea what they'd thought of me at all. I didn't know how many other girls were up for the part, though I did discover that one of those who auditioned was Emma Bunton, who later found fame with the Spice Girls. I knew there would be fierce competition, but I couldn't help hoping that this would be my big break, my chance to show what I could really do, to give Charley some kind of security for his future. It would be all my hopes and dreams rolled into one.

I didn't know how long it would be before I heard from them. I collected Charley from Mum, then went back to my little flat. My friend Simone was staying with me at the time, so she made us a cup of tea while I changed Charley. Then the phone rang. I leaped on it, while Simone watched me, teaspoon in hand. It was Anna.

'You've got the part,' she yelled.

I screamed and started jumping around the room. 'Oh, my God, Simone, I've got it, I've got it,' I shouted.

Simone hugged me and then said, 'Sod the tea, this deserves champagne.' We couldn't afford that, so she rushed out to get a bottle of sparkling wine instead while I rang Mum, who was ecstatic.

When Simone got back we opened the bottle and she handed a couple of glasses to some builders who were on the scaffolding outside our window, working on the flats. 'My friend's just got a part in *EastEnders*,' she told them, and they all laughed and said, 'Well done.'

It was hard to come back to earth. I was being offered a three-month contract, but if I did well it might be extended to a year. I thought about the faces on *EastEnders* that we all knew so well. Would I really be joining them? It seemed terrifying and wildly exciting at the same time.

I spent the next few days in a blur, wildly happy yet trying to calm myself and prepare mentally for the huge change all this would bring. I would be working regularly at least five days a week, and would need to organize childcare and a routine for Charley and me. Soon afterwards things started to get going when I was called to a photo shoot for the whole Jackson clan: the pictures would be issued to the press to introduce the latest troubled family to arrive in the Square. Lindsay Coulson was to play my mum, Carol, and Michael French was to play my dad David Wicks, who was also the son of Pat Evans. Howard Anthony was playing my stepdad, Alan, and I had two half-brothers, Dean Gaffney, playing Robbie, and Devon Anderson who played Billy, the little one. I also had a half-sister, Sonia, played by Natalie Cassidy. I knew Natalie, who was only nine, from Anna Scher's, but the others were all new to me. Nevertheless it didn't take long for us to become friends and start feeling like a real family.

A couple of weeks later I was due to start work

on the set. Because I'd been to Elstree before, for *Grange Hill*, I knew what to do, but I still felt like a little girl on her first day at school. I made a real effort to look nice and got there early. At the gates the security guard asked me who I was and where I was going. I felt like an impostor saying, 'I'm in *EastEnders*,' and thought he'd laugh and tell me to go home. In fact the security people never took much notice of who you were. They were used to stars going in and out each day and treated everyone in the same way—even if they knew exactly who you were, if you didn't have your pass you had to wait at the gate for security clearance. Elstree might have been home to some of the best-known programmes on TV, but it was far from glamorous. In fact it had a decidedly dated air and could have done with a facelift.

I headed for the *EastEnders* building, which was over to the left of the main building, down a short road full of speed bumps. It looked like a giant aircraft hangar, but once I stepped through the door I could see that inside it was divided into a number of different areas. An assistant hastily showed me to make-up and wardrobe, where I had to get ready for the day's scenes. Everywhere I looked there were people rushing about and most of them had no time to stop, though they did give me friendly smiles.

There was an area outside the wardrobe and make-up departments where a lot of the cast members hung about, and as I approached I saw Pam St Clements, who played Pat Evans, Ross Kemp, who played Grant Mitchell, and Steve McFadden, who played his brother Phil, sitting there. I felt completely in awe, but they came over

149

to say hello as I went in.

I wasn't the only new cast member that day—most of the rest of the Jackson family were starting at the same time. My first scene was to be with my screen mum, Lindsay Coulson. As I put on Bianca's over-the-top clothes and had my make-up done I tried to control my nerves. I'd learned my lines and knew the scene, but would I pull it off? I was still afraid that they'd decide I was an impostor and send me back home. On the surface I was smiling and confident, but underneath I couldn't believe I was being accepted as an actress. I'd acted professionally for years but this was my first major role. And after all, many of the cast members had been to prestigious drama schools and had a lot of experience in the theatre. Perhaps it was because I was playing a sixteen-year-old, but I felt like the youngest person there even though I wasn't. I looked up to everyone else and was desperate to be liked and to get everything right.

Once I was ready I was called out on the lot, and was amazed at the smallness of Albert Square. It was so weird seeing the market and the Queen Vic pub for real that I stared open-mouthed at everything like a star-struck kid. My first scene was a huge row in the market with Lindsay, and I was determined to give it my best. I wanted *EastEnders* to represent a fresh start in my life, a chance to create a future for me and for Charley. So I put my heart into it.

After two takes the director was happy, and when we had finished filming everyone on set—the other cast members and the crew—clapped. I had thrown myself into it so completely that I didn't realize they were all watching, and I blushed scarlet. But I was really proud. I had made a good start.

9

FINDING MY FEET

For the next couple of weeks it all seemed very surreal. In past acting jobs I'd started out not knowing my fellow actors and had got to know them over the first few days of filming. But with *EastEnders* it was different. I felt as though I knew everyone already because I'd seen them so often on screen, but when I began work I realized that I didn't know them at all. The actors were often so different from their screen characters, and I had to undo any image I had of them and start all over again. I felt very shy with most of the cast, although I made an effort to appear confident and cheerful. If anyone asked me how I was I'd smile brightly and say, 'Fine', no matter how I really felt. Characters like Phil and Grant were very familiar to me, but actors Steve McFadden and Ross Kemp were strangers. Both of them, however, were incredibly kind and welcoming, as were all the rest of the cast. Some of them took longer to get to know than others. It was a while before Wendy Richard, who played Pauline Fowler, warmed to me, but eventually we became good friends.

Because I'd worked at Elstree before I knew my way to the canteen and so on, but it was still daunting to be there playing a new character in a peak-time rolling drama. It was Sid Owen who made all the difference. We were already friends, and once we were working together we became very close. After so many years he knew it all, showed me where I needed to be and spent a lot of time with me when we weren't on set. Sid was, and is, a lovely person and is still one of my best friends.

Soon after I started work I told the senior executives—and then everyone else—about Charley. I had been afraid that being a single mum would count against me in some way, but once I started work I realized my fears were probably groundless. When I plucked up the courage to tell everyone they were lovely and told me to bring him in as soon as possible so that they could all meet him.

I was thrilled to be given a dressing room to myself, even though they were just tiny cells in a large Portakabin. They were all painted magnolia, but I was allowed to do mine over in peppermint green which I thought made it much nicer. It contained a little bed, which I often used for a kip at lunchtime or when I wasn't needed, and I put pictures of Charley and my friends round the mirror and on the walls. Sid's dressing room was next door, so we spent a lot of time between takes together; and sometimes, when we were onset together, we used to get the giggles so badly that we were called to the production office and told off like naughty children. No doubt we deserved it, but despite our fooling around we both worked hard and never got a line wrong. When we heard that our characters were going to get together, and eventually marry, it meant we got to act a lot of our scenes together and it seemed perfect.

Mike Reid was another very funny man. In between takes behind the bar of the Vic he'd do a stand-up comedy routine and have us all in stitches. The trouble was, if you were in a scene where you were supposed to be upset you'd have only a couple of seconds between Mike's last joke and the director's shout of 'Action' to get yourself back in character. Sometimes I giggled so much at Mike or Sid that I wanted to cry. It was the best and the worst feeling in the world—I enjoyed it, but sometimes I couldn't stop. If Mike wasn't cracking jokes Sid would be corpsing me, or else Todd Carty, who played Mark Fowler and also loved a joke, would give me a look which set me off again.

I soon got into the routine of leaving Charley with Mum each morning, going to work and then collecting Charley on my way home in the evening. I didn't socialize with the other actors outside work. We got to know each other well, but at the end of the working day we all went off to our own homes and our own lives.

The episodes were shown six weeks after we filmed them, so I'd already got used to the routine, the set and the cast by the time my first scene was shown in November 1993. I watched it at home with Mum and the rest of the family. They all loved it when I came on, but I hated seeing myself. I didn't like my voice and I thought my acting was awful. Through all my years in *EastEnders* I never really got used to seeing myself and mostly I didn't watch if I was on, though I loved seeing everyone else in the show. We were so busy with our own parts that we missed a lot of what everyone else was doing, so I'd watch the show in order to catch up!

Shortly before that first scene appeared Anna Scher took me out to lunch. She told me that this was different from any job I'd done before, and that a lot was going to change for me once I was appearing regularly. She warned me that the press would be interested in me and that I needed to be careful and to keep my feet on the ground.

I had no idea what she was talking about. I never read the papers and had no idea of the kind of coverage *EastEnders* got. I loved the idea of having my picture taken and being in the papers, although I couldn't seriously imagine that anyone would be interested in me. I was utterly naïve and had no idea that I might be famous and no understanding of the pressures fame might bring. All I could think was *What's Anna going on about? It all sounds fantastic to me.*

In fact the press interest in me began even before I appeared on screen. I was asked to a film premiere in Romford—a smallish event—and a journalist from the local paper was there. I told her I was going to be in *EastEnders*, and the next day my picture was in the national press as the new face in the show. It gave me a shock. Why would they want to use a picture of me before anyone even knew who I was? But that was just the first drop in what would prove to be a torrent of publicity. Within days of my first appearance I was getting requests from magazines and newspapers for photo shoots and interviews.

The BBC was fine about publicity, because it was good for the show, so I happily agreed to some of the requests. But I had no idea what I was letting myself in for. One Sunday paper wanted to take pictures of me in a little lacy see-though top. I felt very uneasy, but I put it on when they promised that the flash of the camera meant that it wouldn't appear see-though in the picture. After the shoot I became really worried that I'd been an idiot, so I told Anna. She rang the paper and explained that I was very new to the business and asked them not to use the pictures. Thankfully they only used one or two of the less revealing ones.

On another occasion I wasn't so lucky. Some pictures that surfaced in another Sunday paper, taken when I was sixteen, were glamour shots I'd agreed to do for a friend's art college project. She had to take all kinds of different photos and asked me if I'd help her out with the glamour ones. I thought it was a laugh, so I posed topless with a cigar and a teddy bear. Afterwards I forgot all about it—the pictures had been private and I knew my friend would never do anything with them. But what I'd forgotten was that I'd given a couple to a boyfriend, who must now have realized he could make a bit of money with them.

I was at a friend's house on the Sunday morning when the pictures appeared. I was asleep in the spare room when her dad called round to drop something off, and woke to hear his voice in the hall saying, 'I can't believe it—look at little Julie with her tits out!' I sat bolt upright in bed, completely shocked, and couldn't think what he was on about. Until I saw the paper in question I'd completely forgotten about the shoot all those years ago. Absolutely mortified, I rushed back home and hid for the rest of the day. On set next day no one said a thing. Just about every member of the cast knew what it was like to be stitched up by the press, so there was nothing but silent sympathy.

Soaps are half-drama, half-tabloid, and publicity is an integral part of being in one. In the early days I rarely said no to requests for photo shoots and interviews because it was all part of what was expected, or at least I felt it was, and I was very eager to please. It was only later that I realized I could afford to be more choosy.

Despite the enormous press interest in *EastEnders*, and in some of the characters in particular, there were no star egos there. We were actors doing a job, and that's how we saw ourselves. Even the most popular and successful actors were totally down to earth, and there were no big heads or tantrums. Impressed by everyone's professionalism, I was determined not to let any of them down. I could see that the actors who coped best were the ones who kept their feet on the ground and had families to go home to. Adam Woodyat, who plays Ian Beale, was a lovely man, funny, kind and easy to talk to. He worked hard, then went home to his family and never let any of the hype fool him. He knew it was just a job and I learned a lot from watching people like him and Todd Carty, who was very similar in attitude. Steve McFadden (Phil Mitchell) was another truly nice guy, great fun to be with and an excellent actor who taught me a lot.

There was a crèche at the studios and I started bringing Charley in sometimes to give Mum a break. More often than not, though, I didn't need the crèche, because lots of people were happy to play with him while I filmed. I'd often be in the middle of an Albert Square scene and out of the corner of my eye see Charley being cuddled in the arms of one of the crew. The producer, Jane Harris, was a warm, friendly woman whose relaxed style made working on the show so much more fun. She didn't mind Charley being around the set, and from time to time she even let me bring friends in to act as extras in scenes in the Queen Vic or the Square.

At the end of my three-month contract I was offered another for a year, with an option for a further year, which of course meant that if I did my job well I'd got work for the next two years. I was so happy: they liked me, they wanted me to stay and my future, for the moment, looked perfect. I celebrated by going out and buying myself a four-door Ford Fiesta in racing green—very cool. Once I had my long-term contract I began to feel I really belonged. At the beginning it had felt like a dream and I'd been sure I'd wake up and find I wasn't really in *EastEnders* at all. But now, as time went by, I became less in awe of the established cast members and more confident about my ability as an actress and my place in the cast.

At that time *EastEnders* was only on twice a week, and we had time for rehearsals. But six months after I arrived the number of episodes was increased to three and there was no time for rehearsals any more—we just had to learn the script and go straight to filming. This was made even harder by the fact that inside scenes were shot one week and outside ones the next. This meant that, if you were doing a scene in the café and then walked out and carried on the scene outside, you had to shoot it in two parts. You might have to be in a real state about something, then cut and get back to the same scene a week later, picking up where you had left off, wearing the same clothes and re-creating the same emotional state. It could be a huge challenge, but I loved it. In fact from the start I loved everything about being in *EastEnders*. I was determined to create a good character and stay as long as they'd have me. I learned my lines every night, no matter what else I was up to, and made sure I was always in on time and knew what I should be doing.

I knew how lucky I was, and how many actresses would have loved the break I'd been given. But that wasn't enough to stop me partying or taking drugs. I was just determined to manage things so that my drug-taking never got in the way of my work. I was still going out and taking huge amounts of Ecstasy, vomiting all over dance floors and then taking more drugs. My face was so well known by then that it's amazing no one recognized me and told the press, but somehow I got away with it. There were many times when I arrived at work in the morning after partying—and being off my head on drugs—all night. I'd shower and change before appearing on set, and when the lunch break came I'd grab a Mars bar and a Coke and then have a sleep on the bed in my dressing room.

Sometimes I was still high on Ecstasy when I got to work, but I don't think anyone realized—they thought my exuberant moods were natural. I remember Pam St Clements—a gorgeous woman, classy, wise and always a friend—saying to me, 'You're such a happy little thing, aren't you?' If only she'd known—but she was far too kind and trusting to have had any idea that my high spirits were chemically induced.

Jane Harris must have noticed me looking a

little the worse for wear, because she called me into her office a few times to ask whether I was all right. 'Are you getting enough sleep?' she said. 'What are you doing outside work?' She was probably used to young cast members burning the candle at both ends, but was only ever kind and polite. I assured her that everything was fine, and she asked me to promise to come and see her if I had any problems. I promised, but laughed to myself. *What does she mean? I don't have any problems*, I thought.

Looking back, I'm amazed at my degree of denial and the way I fooled everyone—most of all myself. And I don't know how I kept going. Sometimes I think, *How am I not dead?*, given the drink, drugs, lack of sleep, lack of proper nutrition and non-stop schedule that I inflicted on myself. My addictions meant that I hardly ever ate properly, because I just wasn't hungry. With no idea how to look after myself I often got through the day on a Coke and a couple of chocolate bars. I was always skinny, and the press often reported that I had anorexia. In fact I never did—I simply had no appetite and just didn't care about food. I'm not proud of the way I behaved, or what I did to myself; in fact I cringe when I think about it. Perhaps the reason I got away with it was so that I could help others by stopping them from doing what I did.

I may have been twenty-two with an enviable career, an adorable baby son and a great salary, but I was still emotionally immature and behaving in a way that was both sad and foolish. But I had, of course, never felt good about myself deep inside, and no amount of outer success was going to change that. The drugs to which I resorted

159

achieved nothing but a vicious circle, and my constant anxiety meant that since childhood I had never been able to face being alone. As a result I made sure I was always with other people, even when I had to throw drugs parties to keep them with me.

In addition to all this I was still struggling with being a mum, despite my pride in Charley. When I wasn't out partying I would collect him from the Elstree crèche, or from Mum's, and go home to my little flat. I'd feed him and put him to bed, make my own supper and curl up in front of the TV. But I didn't feel at ease—in fact I was constantly on edge, scared that someone would try to break in. This was another manifestation of my anxiety and fear, which hadn't been helped by the mugging when I was fourteen. I'd had bars put on the windows and doors, but I still felt afraid. And I was restless, which probably had a lot to do with the drugs still coursing through my veins. Every night before going to bed I'd smoke a joint to try to help me get to sleep. I took sleeping tablets too—I was so scared living alone that I just couldn't sleep. But sometimes nothing worked and I lay awake half the night. And after a couple of nights like this I was desperate to get out again and lose myself in drugs.

Nicole, the good friend I'd had since primary school, did her best to help and support us both as did her boyfriend Jason. I was absolutely devastated when I heard that Jason had been killed in a tragic accident: he was going over to Belgium on the ferry when the gangway collapsed as he was boarding. It was a terrible loss for Nicole, who was inconsolable—and for Charley and me too, because Jason had been an important part of our lives. He was only twenty-eight and I just couldn't believe he was gone. I wanted to make it better for Nicole, but I knew I couldn't and I felt helpless.

Jason's death only fuelled my craving for oblivion from my feelings even more. There had been such a lot of losses in my life—Dad, Norah, May and, in a way, Albert—that I had never truly grieved over. But once again I pushed the feelings away, handed Charley to Mum and hit the clubs and the comfort of the false high. I invited people back to my flat to party afterwards so often, and we made such a noise, that the neighbours complained and the environmental health department of the local council tried to get me thrown out. The lady downstairs would bang on the ceiling with her broom to the beat of the music we had on, which was often Mariah Carey's 'Dream Lover' or 'It's Not Over'. I loved my music—if I hadn't been an actress I'd like to have been a disc jockey. Music lifts me like nothing else, and I still have a huge passion for it.

I knew I ought to attempt to lead a more normal life, and a handful of times I tried. I'd ask a girlfriend to come and stay with me at the flat, so that I wouldn't be alone, and I'd live quietly for a few weeks, trying to stick to work and looking after Charley. But my girlfriends couldn't stay indefinitely, and as soon as they left I'd be painfully lonely again. I didn't want to mess things up further—for Charley's sake I wanted to succeed and make a good life. But I didn't know how.

It was a sad way to live, and I feel especially sad when I think how long I let it carry on. At those moments when I realized just what a mess I was in and how badly I needed help, I always pushed away the thought and reached for more drugs. They were my answer to everything. I feel sorry about the time I missed with Charley, too. Because none of my girlfriends had children I felt like the odd one out, and all too often I asked Mum to look after him while I escaped into the party life I had revelled in before I became a single mother.

I never took drugs when I was with Charley. If I let him down it was by not being with him enough of the time, and so missing out on the intimate bond between mother and child. I feel sad because, although Charley and I are now close, that time can never be replaced. And I'm very grateful that, although I wasn't always there, Charley had such a strong, secure environment with Mum, Ted and the rest of our family and friends giving him attention and loving him. As a result of that he wasn't aware of the excesses of my lifestyle.

Somehow I got away with it—for a while, at least. And in *EastEnders* I was being given strong storylines that really challenged and excited me. My first screen kiss was with an actor called Ian Reddington, who played the shifty market inspector known as Tricky Dickie. He was quite a bit older than me and I was terribly nervous and embarrassed about having to kiss him. And it wasn't just a quick peck, either, but a full snog. But I did it, and afterwards he teased me and we had a laugh. Next Bianca tried to seduce David Wicks, not knowing that he was actually her father. But despite her interest in older men, Bianca's true love was mechanic Ricky. Not that Bianca and Ricky didn't have their ups and downs. There were a number of times when it looked as though it would all be called off. There was Ricky's affair with Natalie Evans, Bianca's best friend, which resulted in Bianca driving Natalie out of town. The episode in February 1995 in which Bianca discovered Ricky was cheating on her with Natalie drew an audience of 17 million. And Ricky wasn't the only one who was unfaithful. Bianca had a one-night stand with barman Lenny Wallace, played by Desune Coleman, which led to a pregnancy scare and once again almost ended her relationship with Ricky.

But despite all the hiccups, when Ricky and Bianca became a couple they seemed to enter the nation's consciousness. As Bianca I often shouted (or should that be screeched?) 'Rickeeee' at Sid on screen, and off screen everywhere either of us went it was screeched back at us by laughing members of the public. Neither of us minded—we were flattered that people liked our characters so much and felt they knew us. People still do it now, years after Bianca and Ricky disappeared from *EastEnders*.

I was loving my role, and my time on the show, so it was a cruel blow when health problems forced me to take an unscheduled break. I was out shopping with Mum one day when I suddenly bent double with the most awful pain, so bad that I could hardly speak. Mum got me into a taxi and took me to hospital, where I was given all kinds of tests and kept in for two days, which I hated. They told me it was a grumbling appendix and that I wouldn't need an operation as it would settle down. I was on painkillers for a few days and after that I felt fine. But three months later, in October 1995, I collapsed again, on an outing to the cinema with Charley and some friends. Once again I was taken to hospital, and this time they said my appendix would have to come out. I had to spend two weeks recovering, which meant the *EastEnders* scripts had to be rewritten because at that time I was appearing in almost every episode. I felt terrible for letting them down, even though I couldn't help it— I hated missing work and sat miserably at home, worrying that they'd decide they didn't need me any more. There was still a tiny part of me that felt I wasn't good enough and would one day be found out and told to leave. So it was a relief when I was welcomed back and Sid and I were plunged straight into the will they/won't they romance between Bianca and Ricky which kept viewers guessing for months on end.

10

FAME

I didn't often socialize with the cast since most of them went straight home after work, but there were a couple of exceptions. Sid and I often saw one another, of course, and I became good friends with Lucy Speed, who played Natalie and sometimes came home with me after work. We'd run through our lines for the next day and then go out for a drink or to a club. Lucy was really good fun, and I missed her when she left *EastEnders* just over a year after I joined.

Martine McCutcheon arrived a year after me. She was only eighteen, yet looked totally confident. I was amazed that someone so young could be so sure of herself—it didn't occur to me that she might have been putting on a front. We weren't friends for a long time—I was so wrapped up in my own role and my friendship with Sid that I didn't do enough at the outset to put her at her ease. In any case, Martine had been trained at the Italia Conti, and I used to look at her waltzing around and think, *She's a right little stage school Sally, showing off to everyone.*

She played Bianca's close friend Tiffany Raymond, breezing in from a stay in Spain. In her first scene she had to go to the Albert Square fish and chip shop with Bianca, where they bumped into Ricky. Bianca suggested a night out for the three of them, and Tiffany responded with a catty remark to Ricky who she thought was rather pathetic. Despite her nerves Martine pulled it off beautifully, and I could see she was going to be very good. As we were playing best friends Martine and I naturally had a lot of scenes together, but our friendship didn't develop until she'd been on the show for a couple of years. It took me a while to see what a truly nice person she is, and that as well as being stunningly pretty she was warm, funny and a loyal friend.

When we did talk honestly to one another we realized we were very similar—both of us had arrived at *EastEnders* feeling scared and making a brave show of appearing far more self-possessed than we really were. I used to be so anxious about looking like an idiot that I'd pretend to know all kinds of things I didn't. Sitting in make-up or waiting between scenes, some of the cast would start talking about Shakespeare, playwrights, novels or films. I hadn't usually heard of any of them, but

165

I'd nod my head knowingly or murmur agreement. It was Lindsay Coulson who gave me a piece of advice I have never forgotten. She took me aside one day and said, 'Patsy, you never have to pretend you know if you don't. Don't be afraid to say, "I don't know." We all think we *should* know, but most of the time most of us don't.' Lindsay too became a friend, and when I introduced her to my brother Harry, who had by then trained as a psychotherapist, they hit it off immediately—so much so that a few years later, much to my delight, they got married.

Despite the breakneck speed of life on the *EastEnders* set as we raced to pack as many scenes as possible into each day, there was a lot of humour and friendly banter and behind the scenes we had great fun. *Top of the Pops* was filmed in another Elstree studio, and lots of actors and musicians went backwards and forwards between the two. One day I met one of my heroes, Stevie Wonder, who touched my hair and told me it felt wonderful. I was standing in the corridor with Howard Anthony, who played my stepfather Alan, the day I met Stevie. We were so thrilled to meet him that we asked someone to run back to our set to get a camera, and we kept Stevie chatting until that person got back. It was a Polaroid camera, so we thought we'd be able to see our photos straightaway. It was then that we realized there was no film in it. We were so embarrassed we didn't tell Stevie, who had already been so generous with his time—we couldn't possibly have kept him there any longer. At least I had had a special moment with him, and I cherish that memory. I went to see him play at the Royal Albert Hall soon after that, and he was brilliant.

In those days Robbie Williams was still in Take That and they were on *Top of the Pops* every other week as they kept getting hit after hit. Robbie loved *EastEnders*, so he used to come over from their studio to ours to watch and we got friendly. He'd hang out in my dressing room and we'd chat about his life with the band and mine in the soap. Robbie was dying to appear in it, so one day I asked Jane if my friend could be in a scene as an extra. She said he could, and Robbie, delighted, was filmed in the background talking on the phone behind the bar in the Queen Vic. We wondered whether anyone would have recognized him—of course they had, and the day after the scene appeared the story was in all the papers.

Robbie wasn't the only pop star who loved *EastEnders*. One day I saw Noel Gallagher in the canteen carrying a tray full of egg and chips—Oasis were appearing on *Top of the Pops*. He bounded over to tell me how much he loved me in the show, then went down on one knee—still holding his egg and chips—and asked me to marry him!

On another occasion a friend of mine asked me if he could bring his new girlfriend round to my flat to see me. A few days later he appeared with a pretty, dark-haired girl whom he introduced as Victoria. She told me she loved me in *EastEnders* and wanted to know how to handle fame and the press. 'I'm in an all-girl band and I think we're going to be big,' she confided. 'I need to know how to handle it.'

I told her there was no secret to it—you just had to keep your head down and get on with things. 'You're bound to get the odd bit of publicity you don't like,' I told her, 'but you have to smile and pretend you don't mind. It comes with the job.'

We chatted for a couple of hours. I thought she was a sweet girl, but I wondered if she was right to be so confident about her band. 'What are they called?' I asked as she was leaving.

'The Spice Girls,' she smiled.

A few months later their debut single, 'Wannabee', hit the charts and the Spice Girls were everywhere. When they performed on *Top of the Pops* I bumped into Victoria again. Charley was four by then, and she played with him and gave him cuddles. He met all the other girls, too, and had his photo taken with them—great playground cred for him at that time!

Those were wonderful days, with bands like Take That, Oasis and the Spice Girls all on the up and *EastEnders* at a tremendous peak. We all felt we were a part of Britain's up-and-coming talent, and it was great. I was becoming increasingly well known, and it amazes me, when I look back, that I managed to continue with my habit and remain very much a part of the drug culture while at the same time presenting a glamorous public face as Patsy Palmer, *EastEnders* star. How I did it without being found out I don't know—I would go straight from some awards ceremony or public function to a drug party back home, without giving a thought to the strange contrast in lifestyles or the fact that I might be spotted by the press. I took some ridiculous risks, even taking drugs in nightclubs where I could easily have been recognized, but somehow got away with it and kept my career intact. I was careful in some ways, though. I didn't turn up to public functions appearing drugged or drunk. I knew that if my eyes were glazed or I was weaving about the story would be in every newspaper next day, so I made sure that I did my drug-taking after such events and not before.

By this time I was regularly seeing my face on magazine covers. It felt odd at first, but I soon got used to it. And I began to enjoy getting the star treatment and being asked to attend almost every celebrity event in London, not to mention meeting many of my childhood heroes. I didn't always go— it would have been impossible—but some of the events I was asked to were fabulous. Not long after I joined *EastEnders* I was invited to a show at the London Hippodrome called *The Night of 200 Stars*. The host was Hollywood actor Robert Wagner and the guests included Ginger Rogers, a living legend, who came along in a wheelchair, bless her. Vivienne Westwood had offered me one of her outfits to wear, and I jumped at the chance. She never goes in for quiet little numbers, and she didn't disappoint that night. I arrived, in company with my mum, feeling like a million dollars in a shimmering gold evening dress topped by a gold cape.

Robert Wagner began his introduction and then said, 'I'd like to introduce some of our special guest stars.' Like everyone else I craned around to see who they were, and suddenly I heard him say, 'Patsy Palmer.' I was stunned. Everyone clapped and cheered and Mum dissolved into tears. I wasn't sure what to do, so I half stood up and smiled before sinking back into my seat scarlet with embarrassment.

My first awards ceremony was around this time too. In November 1995 I was nominated for Best

Newcomer in the first National Television Awards. Robbie Williams was the host and I saw him at Elstree after he'd been in rehearsal for it. He bounced up to me, all enthusiasm and boyish grin, and said, 'You've won! I've just been reading out, ". . . and the winner is . . . Patsy Palmer".' I nearly had a heart attack. How was I going to handle it? I threw myself into preparations, rehearsing my acceptance speech, getting my hair and make-up done specially and acquiring a gorgeous wine-coloured Vivienne Westwood suit with wedges which made me tower over everyone—though I was very nervous about falling down the steps from the stage. Most of the ceremony passed in a blur as I waited for my moment. At last Robbie opened the envelope. He even looked at me and gave me a little wink. My heart pounded. Then Robbie, the shock clear on his face, read out, '. . . and the winner is . . . Angela Griffin for *Coronation Street*'. I already had my bum half off my seat when I heard those words. Neither Robbie nor I knew what had happened until afterwards, when he came and found me and apologized profusely. 'It turns out they just give us any of the names during rehearsals,' he said. 'They keep the real winner secret.'

It didn't matter in the least. We laughed about it, and I learned never to take anything for granted again. I was very lucky, because in subsequent awards ceremonies I did make it to the winner's podium a few times and even when I didn't, sometimes the nomination itself felt like a terrific achievement. For instance, I was very honoured and excited to be the first-ever soap character to be nominated (for Best Actor—Female) in the prestigious Royal Television Society awards. For these, people within the television industry choose the nominees and from that shortlist vote for the winners, so it felt like a vote of confidence from fellow professionals. And although I didn't win I received a certificate just for being nominated, which doesn't usually happen.

EastEnders itself, of course, was winning awards every year, and we all had a lot of fun going along to the ceremonies. While I was in it the show won Best Popular Drama in the National Television Awards for 1995, 1996 and 1997, which was an enormous thrill for everyone involved.

As well as the fantastic invitations, the chance to wear wonderful designer clothes and the awards, there were other great perks. I was invited to go and have my hair done by Daniel Galvin at his West End salon, and I jumped at the chance. Nicole Kidman, Patsy Kensit and a host of other stars went there. Throughout my time on *EastEnders* Daniel or his son James did my hair, blow-drying it straight as it had a bit of a kink which I didn't like. It was very long then, and incredibly thick—the Galvins said it was the thickest hair they'd ever done. It became quite a talking point in the business. There was even some discussion, at one point, about me doing a commercial for a major hair products manufacturer, and six-figure sums were bandied about. It all fell through when the BBC said I couldn't do it, which I suppose was fair enough since they didn't even carry commercials, but it was still a bit disappointing.

There were some unusual and bizarre consequences to fame, too. One of the oddest happened about eighteen months after I joined *EastEnders*, when I accidentally got caught up in Ronnie Kray's funeral. Ronnie was one of the notorious Kray twins, who with their older brother Charlie were among the East End's most powerful and menacing villains. I was on the way to a sunbed appointment in the snazzy little Jeep I'd bought (the Fiesta was soon upgraded) when I turned into a road that was blocked by a crowd of hundreds of people. I couldn't see what was going on so I got out and sat on the roof of my car, waiting to find out. Suddenly a photographer snapped me, but I still had no idea what was going on. Eventually someone told me what it was all about. I had to wait ages to get through, and I missed my appointment by several hours.

The next day the papers published a picture of me with the headline: 'Patsy attends Ronnie Kray's funeral'. Totally untrue, but there was nothing I could do. It got worse when I received a message from Ronnie's twin Reggie, who was still in prison, telling me how touched he was that I'd attended his brother's funeral and asking me to visit him. I was so embarrassed—and rather alarmed as well. I had to send a message back saying my stepdad didn't really like me going into prisons so I was very sorry but I couldn't come.

Though I loved the celebrity lifestyle and the perks and treats that came with it I was still most at home with my old friends, and I preferred to party with them. We'd go out clubbing as ever, but increasingly now I was recognized and fans would drive me mad, coming up to me all the time. Because of this we'd usually end up having house parties, where I could relax and be out of the public eye.

I always thought I knew what I was doing, but I seldom did. I often took drugs without even knowing what they were, which might seem odd given that I was fearful of so many other aspects of life and one night this carelessness almost killed me. A party was in full swing at my flat, and a friend and I were driving around looking for somewhere to pick up more drugs. I was in my pyjamas and buzzing out of my head—I'd already taken about five Ecstasy pills over the course of the evening, not to mention alcohol, marijuana and cocaine. Eventually we heard that we could get some at a house in Southgate in north London.

When we got there we were offered some odd little green pills. We weren't sure what they were—no one seemed to know—but in our already drugged state we thought that was funny and decided to take a bag of them back to the party in my flat. Nowadays I can hardly believe the casual way I downed unidentified drugs as if they were Smarties, but that's what addiction does to you. Before we left I rolled another joint and we smoked it. Then I stood up to leave, and as I did so I put one of the little green pills in my mouth. After a few seconds my head felt as if it was going to explode, and I collapsed on the floor unconscious. My friend picked me up and started slapping my face and shouting, 'Wake up! Come on, babe, wake up!'

Thank God I did, after a few minutes. But it gave the people in the house a big fright—they were about to call an ambulance. I never found out what I had taken, but the sensation in my head, both before and after I passed out, was like nothing

I had ever experienced before and I believe that had I taken two pills instead of one—as I might easily have done—I wouldn't have survived. As it was, I recovered—and, astonishingly, I just shrugged it off and carried on partying.

I took foolish risks many times, and was very, very lucky not to have done myself permanent damage or taken an accidental overdose. Some of the people around me were just as reckless and had their own brushes with death, but none of these experiences scared us enough to stop us. We laughed about them, thinking it was cool and clever to live on the edge. Now when I hear about young people dying after taking drugs—sometimes far smaller quantities than I regularly took—I feel terribly sad and very aware that there, but for the kindness of fate, go I.

I may have been totally irresponsible with drink and drugs, but I was quite careful with my money. Ever since I'd started playing Bianca I'd been saving most of my salary. I dreamed of having a home of my own instead of a rented flat, and after two years I was finally able to afford one: a little terraced two-bedroom house in Jesus Green in Bethnal Green. It wasn't my first choice—I'd seen another little house before that in Quilter Street, which seemed perfect. But I was gazumped by the producers of Mike Leigh's film *Secrets and Lies*, who bought the house to film in. I had always wanted to be in a Mike Leigh film so I took to walking up and down outside the house, hoping he would notice me. When that didn't work I drove up and down outside with loud music blaring, hoping to really annoy him. I was very cross about losing the house and decided that if I couldn't get a part in his film then pissing him off was the next best choice. Sadly immature, I know. And years later I met Mike Leigh, who told me he'd love to work with me—so who knows? We may make it one day.

The Jesus Green house may have been my second choice, but after the grim little flat it seemed wonderful. Charley had his own bedroom for the first time and I decorated it in blue for him. Then I got a local artist to paint a castle and clouds on the ceiling and safari murals on his wardrobe. I went slightly over the top everywhere, with all kinds of paint effects and colours I thought were great but that would probably make me wince now. We were only just round the corner from Mum, so we still spent as much time at her house as at our own. I often used to pop round for tea, and dropped Charley off whenever I went out. But in my new house I felt much safer than I had in the flat, so I was happier spending time there. And I felt very grown up—I was proud of having earned the money to buy it.

Around this time my mum's father, Farvy, died. He'd come through so much, and had so many things wrong with him, that I'd always believed he was invincible. It was lung cancer that got him in the end. We all loved Farvy, and laughed about the things he came out with. Mum was a bit scared of him—not surprisingly, since she'd seen his violent side—but I wasn't; I could be very cheeky to him and he'd just laugh. I was his little princess, the granddaughter who could do no wrong, and although he had his dark side, to me he was always generous and loving. He was also ridiculously over-protective of me, and still wouldn't let me touch a hot kettle when I was twenty-five! And he used to tell Mum that I didn't know what I was doing with Charley and would drop him.

Farvy died at the age of seventy-five, ten years after Norah, his wife, in the London Hospital in Whitechapel. Mum was visiting him that day, and was expecting his usual moaning and cursing about having to be in hospital. Instead, when she arrived she found him dead in bed and none of the staff had noticed. It was a terrible shock for Mum, who became hysterical.

I came back from the *EastEnders* set that day to find Harry waiting for me. He just cuddled me and said, 'Farvy's dead.' I felt so sad that I went round to Mum's house, and sat on the sofa and cried. I still miss his loud voice and foul language, and I often laugh when I think what an old tyrant he could be. He was so proud of me. He used to sit at his little table in the front room, his teapot—with an old china cup for a lid—in front of him, watching me in *EastEnders*. He'd turned his flat into a shrine, with photos of me all over the place. I loved that—it made me feel really special.

A few years after he died I visited the cemetery to have a few words with him and Nor. I had no idea where they'd put his ashes, as I'd hated the thought of him being cremated and hadn't wanted to see them scattered. I knew Mum had chosen a tree for them and I wandered around the cemetery looking for it, but as there was no plaque or anything to identify it I didn't know where to begin. So I phoned Mum, who described the exact location, and I discovered that I was standing right beside the tree in question. I've always believed that Farvy and Norah are looking out for me. I was so upset that Norah never saw Charley, but after his birth I had a vivid dream in which she said, 'It's OK, Ju. I've seen him.' I was sure it was a sign from her and I felt a deep sense of calm and reassurance.

11

BREAKDOWN

By 1996 my brother Albert had been clean of drink and drugs for some months, and was living in Bristol. At the time it seemed as though his latest stay in rehab had worked, and of course we were all delighted. For Mum, in particular, it was a huge relief and we all hoped desperately that Albert would manage to stay clean and make himself a good life with a job, a relationship and a home.

Sadly, as on every other occasion, Albert went back to taking drugs and his life once again fell apart. As this pattern continued year after year—it does to this day—Albert distanced himself increasingly from us, and in truth we did the same from him. We all told him that we will always support his recovery, but in the end the emotional rollercoaster of trying to get him off drugs, only to see him go back to them, became too emotionally exhausting. Mum, while never giving up on Albert, realized that she had to take a step back from him and from the anxiety and fear she felt for him if she was to live her own life. As any relative of an addict will know, the struggle to help them can become all-consuming and impossible to maintain in the long term without a huge toll on the rest of one's life.

As for me, when Albert was clean I was really pleased, but I didn't relate it in any way to my own drug-taking. I still believed that Albert was an addict and that I wasn't, and there seemed to me to be a huge divide between what he was doing with heroin, which was serious, and what I was doing with 'recreational' drugs, which was fun. It was to be several more years before I understood that Albert and I both suffered from the disease of addiction and that our struggle was the same.

It was easy for me to stay in denial because on the surface there were real differences between the two of us. I had my own home, my lovely son and a great job, while Albert was never in a position to find those things and was in and out of rehab. In time I too would find myself in rehab and on the brink of losing everything I had, but back in 1996 I was still riding a wave of success and nurturing a belief in my own invincibility.

What I wanted at that time was a man in my life: there hadn't been anyone special since Charlie's birth four years earlier. Of course I'd had the odd romance—I even went on holiday to Spain with a boyfriend at one point—but they didn't work out and most of the time I preferred to be on my own. After my early disastrous experiences with men I was determined to avoid obsessing over anyone ever again. I wanted a grown-up relationship, and soon after my twenty-fourth birthday I met someone who seemed to be just what I was looking for.

I'd first met Nick Love a few years earlier, when Albert brought him home to Mum's. The two had known each other since they were teenagers, and were good friends. The only time I'd seen Nick in the five or six years since then was on posters—he was a model for Ralph Lauren and appeared on posters all over London.

After one of his visits to us Albert asked me to drop him at Victoria Station to get a coach back to Bristol, but first he said he wanted to meet Nick to catch up.

I knew Nick had gone to film school and become a director, and thought meeting up with him would make a nice change. I loved the idea of someone so different from the boys I had grown up with—so many of them seemed to have become gangsters and drug dealers, or were in and out of prison. And so many had died unexpectedly. I still grieved for my good friend Jason, and had been terribly shocked when another boy I knew had been stabbed to death in a fight. He'd been a friend since we were kids in Bethnal Green and we still hung out together. He left behind a beautiful girlfriend and a child, and his death seemed such a waste. Another boy I knew had died in a scooter accident soon afterwards. I found it hard to cope with these deaths of such young people, and deep down I was afraid of losing someone too. I didn't want to get involved with someone only to see him die in some pointless way. Apart from that, I felt the life I was leading myself was going nowhere and I became very morbid. I dreamed of my funeral, and became obsessed by thoughts that I would be the next to die a violent death. Curiously, I never worried about the real danger—that I might die through taking drugs. It was the violence and crime I wanted to get away from, and I longed to find something different.

Albert and I met Nick that day in a café called the Dome, and had a coffee together. He had just made a short film he was very proud of, and he told us all about it. I really liked the fact that he had something going on in his life, something he was committed to and passionate about. Afterwards Nick came with us to Victoria. We saw Albert off and then Nick invited me back to his flat in Chelsea, where we spent the afternoon smoking cigarettes, drinking coffee and watching films. Nick showed me a film he'd made about a skinhead, called *Skin*, which I thought was very good. He was—not surprisingly—mad about films, and in particular about the director Martin Scorsese. I enjoyed talking to him because he was knowledgeable and interesting, and it lifted me out of the narrow world I felt I inhabited. At the end of the afternoon I went home feeling fantastic. There had been a real spark between us, which was fun, but it was Nick's passion for his work that made the time I spent with him really special. It opened my eyes to a world in which there was more to life than booze, drugs and partying.

In the following days Nick and I called each other a few times. Then I was given tickets to see a Frank Bruno fight, and invited Nick to come with me. We had front seats and it was a great evening which we both enjoyed. Afterwards we went for something to eat and he told me about the documentary he'd been making with Elton John, called *Tantrums and Tiaras*. He'd been co-producing it with Elton's partner David Furnish, but there had been 'artistic disagreements' and Nick had left before filming was completed. It was fascinating to hear the inside story of film production, and once again I found him great company.

Nick and I began dating after that, crossing London to one another's homes to spend evenings watching films and talking about our lives and our work. From the start Nick was lovely to Charley— they got on so well that Charley would jump up and down with excitement if Nick was coming over. My Mum liked him too, and was delighted that I'd finally met someone outside the East End culture that surrounded me. Nick's family accepted me, too. His mother was a teacher and his father worked for the upmarket men's clothing firm Gieves and Hawkes. They were, therefore, what we always called 'posh', but they never made me feel intimidated: I liked them, and felt they liked me in return.

I knew at an early stage that I wanted the relationship to be serious. I was sure I was ready to settle down and do the family bit, and wanted Nick to move straight in with Charley and me. Nick cared about me, that was certain, but he wanted to take things more slowly and refused to move straight in. And of course he was right. I didn't know it then, but my haste was due far less to being ready to settle down than to my old eagerness to rush in and do too much too soon. I never had known how to pace things—I wanted it all, and I wanted it now.

Despite my impatience and his reluctance, we carried on seeing one another. But there were other big differences between us, too. Nick didn't want to go out raving all night: he wasn't into drink or drugs, and just didn't see the point. I was amazed by his willpower—I'd never met a man who wasn't into those things. Being with someone who didn't use made me think a lot. I knew, deep down, that what I was doing was damaging me, and I wanted to be like Nick; I made the decision then that I would find a way to give up drugs and drink. That decision was momentous because, although it would take me another eight years to beat my addictions, it was the beginning of the end of drugs for me. I had made an internal shift, from believing that drugs were great to knowing that actually they weren't, and that I wouldn't really own my own life until I stopped taking them.

I found myself torn. I still wanted to use, but when I was with Nick I wanted to be like him. We'd go to parties and I'd be falling all over the place while he was sober. Nick was very patient about it and seldom criticized, but one night after I'd downed a load of Ecstasy in a nightclub and was so out of it I barely knew who he was he grabbed me and said, 'What have you taken?' I lied and replied, 'Nothing.' I couldn't bring myself to own up.

But of course he knew. It was obvious when I was on drugs—I'd be happy, buzzy, wanting to party all night, relaxed and full of laughs. Then when I was sober I'd exhibit the classic symptoms of an addict—restless, irritable and anxious. Nick must have cared a lot to put up with all that. I know he worried about me and wanted to help. But he knew what I didn't yet know—that only I could help myself.

One evening he introduced me to a friend of his, a girl, who invited me to come to a Twelve Step meeting with her. I was a bit shocked. I'd been to a Twelve Step meeting with Albert a few years earlier, but that was just to support him. He was the addict, not me. I could stop taking drugs any time I really wanted, I told myself. But Nick's friend was persuasive and I thought, *Why not? No harm in going along.* Even so, I was nervous about going to a meeting in case I was recognized and the press heard about it. What a joke! I didn't worry about being spotted off my head on drugs, but I did worry about being seen trying to come off those drugs.

When I went with Albert I'd thought the whole meeting was a laugh, but this time it was very different. Nick's friend explained that the Twelve Step Programme is about accepting that you have a problem and are powerless to overcome it. Addiction is seen as an illness which stems from a physical allergy that creates uncontrollable cravings for drugs or alcohol. Alongside the physical craving there is a psychological dimension, which means that sufferers keep on rationalizing their relapses. In other words, addicts can't stay away from their addictive substance and will constantly justify, to themselves and others, going back to it. The Twelve Step Programme supports addicts in acknowledging their addiction and in believing that a higher power—God as each person understands him—can restore them to sanity. It involves admitting your shortcomings, making amends to all those you have harmed and learning to face overcoming addiction a day at a time with the help and support of your fellow addicts. Twelve Step meetings exist so that members can share their experiences, support one another and find hope and strength.

This time I didn't giggle. I cried all through the meeting. All the members of the group were women who had problems with drink and drugs, and when they talked about themselves they could just as well have been describing me and my life. One woman talked about her pattern of abusive relationships. Another spoke of her anxiety and how drugs made it go away. Each time I thought, *That's me.* I had never heard other people talk in this way about the kinds of feelings and experiences I lived with every day. But despite this I still wasn't ready to accept, as they had, that I was an addict. My picture of an addict was someone who drank or used from morning till night, who couldn't function, who slept on park benches and queued up at soup kitchens. I had no idea then that this image fits only a tiny minority of addicts and that most are just like me, managing their lives while battling their addiction. So when one or two of the women talked about wanting a fix in the morning I quickly latched on to that and used it as an escape route. *Well, I don't need a fix in the morning,* I thought, *so I'm obviously not like them.*

Nevertheless the meeting had a profound effect on me, and I couldn't stop thinking about how brave and honest these women were. Although I wasn't ready to join them, I did go to a handful of other Twelve Step meetings over the next few months. I observed, rather than joining, but it was a start. Sometimes I saw well-known faces—pop stars, actors and TV presenters. I realized that I wasn't as different or as special as I thought and also that the meetings were safe and private, because none of these people were ever betrayed in the press. The meetings were just what they said they were, anonymous and supportive, so that even if someone was recognized no one would dream of

184

revealing their presence there outside the meeting.

On one occasion I saw a very famous actor. He called me over to sit next to him, and we talked. A humble man who had been sober for a long time, he said, 'You and I have two things to recover from: drink and drug abuse, and ego.' I didn't understand what he meant then, but I have often thought of it since I began my own recovery.

While my private journey towards facing addiction was slow and painstaking, in my work everything was going from strength to strength. At the beginning of March 1997 we filmed Ricky and Bianca's wedding in a church close to Elstree. Word got out, and there were dozens of photographers outside the church and crowds of people lining the street and hanging out of windows to watch. It felt like a royal wedding, and I was the bride in my big white dress. Except that it wasn't real at all, and inside the church Kathy from the wardrobe department had to wrap a coat round me because it was freezing cold, and we were all standing around drinking tea out of polystyrene cups and saying, 'When can we go home?' The wedding episode was shown on 17 April 1997 and had an audience of almost 18 million—one of the biggest ever for a soap.

By the time Nick and I had been together for a year I had managed to stay off drink and drugs for several weeks. I was proud of myself and felt it proved that I wasn't an addict, because I'd done it through sheer willpower, without going into rehab, working the Twelve Steps or anything else. But then I began to suffer from panic attacks. I'd be in the middle of doing something when my hands would start to feel hot and sweaty and I'd feel I couldn't swallow. Then a desperate feeling of anxiety would kick in, I'd get a metallic taste in my mouth, and the feeling that I couldn't swallow would intensify until I was convinced I couldn't breathe and was going to die. It was a horrible, terrifying feeling.

I didn't understand what was going on, or why these attacks were happening with increasing frequency. One day when I was eating dinner in Mum's kitchen I became so convinced I was going to die that I cried for four hours. She told me I was having a panic attack, and comforted me. But neither Mum nor I knew why I was having these attacks, or what to do about them. When the attacks became so frequent that I was having them almost daily I went to the doctor, who organized a brain scan to see if anything was seriously wrong. I half hoped it would be, because I was desperate for an explanation. But the result of the scan was normal. The doctor wanted to put me on anti-depressants. But ironically, considering I was taking just about every non-prescription drug going and was a raging addict, I refused to take them because I was afraid of becoming dependent.

The panic attacks were making me depressed. I felt very low and negative about everything, unmotivated and often tearful. I managed to control the attacks at work, but even there everyone could see that I wasn't well. And the storyline we were filming at that time didn't help.

Not long after the wedding Bianca and Ricky had been told that the baby they were expecting was suffering from spina bifida, an incurable and often terminal condition in which the baby's spine is exposed. A termination was recommended, and

186

reluctantly Bianca agreed. I had to act out Bianca's inconsolable grief, and it was impossible to do it without feeling deeply affected. We filmed one scene in a children's cemetery, which I found extremely hard and emotionally draining. In the past, whenever I had been filming harrowing scenes like this I didn't talk afterwards about how hard it had been and what it had brought up, but just reverted to my normal self as though what I'd just done was nothing out of the ordinary. This was typical of me—I always dealt with painful feelings by ignoring them and carrying on. But now, although I was still struggling to do so, it just wasn't working and the gruelling story I was acting out at work reinforced the depression and panic attacks.

It was Nick who gave me the answer. He'd been giving it to me since the attacks started, but I'd refused to listen. He told me that these were withdrawal symptoms because I'd stopped using drugs. I know now that withdrawal from drugs— any drugs—with no support system in place can lead to an enormous increase in anxiety, which in turn can result in panic attacks. But back then I thought only people on heroin suffered from withdrawal symptoms, and that certainly wasn't me. So I refused to listen to Nick, or even to consider that what he'd said might just be true.

My relationship with him was suffering because of the state I was in. He wanted me to get help from people who understood what I was going through, but I'd stopped going to Twelve Step meetings and refused all his suggestions. In the end Nick decided he'd had enough. I wouldn't listen, I wouldn't get help and I was in such a bad way that he couldn't reach me.

Unable to face what was happening to me, I convinced myself that the answer to all my problems was for Nick to move in with me. I wanted our relationship to become more serious and committed, and thought that when it was I would feel well again. But Nick wasn't ready for that: he wanted to put his energy into his career while I sorted myself out. We were seeing things completely differently, and there was no meeting in the middle. I wasn't ready to listen to him, I knew what I wanted, and if he wouldn't go along with it by moving in—well, nothing else would do. There seemed to be no way forward, so when Nick told me he thought we should split up I agreed. We were too different, and wanted different things. We parted amicably, but inside I was devastated.

Surprisingly even to me, after the split I didn't go straight back to drink and drugs. I was determined to stay clean, even though I'd originally given up because I wanted the relationship with Nick to work. I wasn't about to give in just because he'd left me. But the panic attacks got worse, and a few days later Jane Harris called me into her office at Elstree.

'What's wrong with you?' she asked. 'We can all see something is very wrong.'

I liked and trusted Jane, and told her the truth. I said I'd been on drugs, but that I wasn't any longer. 'I thought I'd feel great,' I told her, 'but I don't. I feel terrible. And on top of that I've just split up with my boyfriend.'

Jane was sympathetic and kind and asked me if I needed time off. But I was sure I didn't. What would I do with myself? I preferred to go to work.

For the next few days I felt in an unreal state. I

was sure I was fine, that everything was fine. But nothing felt quite real—I was going through the motions of my life while floating in space inside my head. Not long after my meeting with Jane, Sid Owen had invited me to go to the Phoenix Music Festival with him and his girlfriend Lucy. I asked my cousin Jackie to go too. We had a great evening, and Sid organized a chauffeur-driven Bentley to take us all home from the airfield outside Stratford-on-Avon where the festival was held. But on the way I began to suffer the worst panic attack of my life.

By the time Sid dropped us off at my house I was struggling to appear normal. Jackie helped me to get to bed, but as I lay there in the dark I started to hear voices—I could hear a man with a Jamaican accent whispering to me. 'I'm going mad—someone's got to help me!' I sobbed. Jackie phoned my brother Harry, who came straight over and stayed with me through the night. It seemed ironic that I had taken so many hallucinogenic drugs and yet had never known the kind of hallucinations I was experiencing now.

By the morning I was calmer and Harry said he would drive me to work. But in the car I began to panic again. 'I can't go to work,' I told him. 'I'm never going there again.'

Harry had known for years about my drug-taking, though not the full extent of it. So many of the people we grew up with took drugs that it wasn't considered shocking or even out of the ordinary. And of course Harry had been involved in the attempts to help Albert over the years, so very little threw him. That morning he realized that I was in a bad way, and his response was brilliant.

189

'Right,' he said. 'I know where you need to go.' He turned the car round and told me to go to sleep because we'd be on the road for a couple of hours. When I woke up we were driving through the gates of a large Victorian country house.

'Where are we?' I asked.

'We're in Kent,' Harry said. 'At the Promis Centre. Where Albert went a few years back. They'll help you here. It's a good place. Don't worry.'

I knew the Promis Centre because I'd visited Albert there. But I didn't need a recovery centre. Or did I? Harry took me inside, and as I stood in the hall I heard him talking to a member of staff. What he said shocked me to the core. 'She needs help,' he told them. 'She's having a breakdown.' Harry stayed to help me register. Albert had been given a government grant to cover the cost of his stay here, but I would have to pay for myself and it wasn't cheap. I didn't care—Harry was right and I needed help. When the forms were filled in Harry gave me a hug and left. As I watched him walk away, a nurse took my arm and led me off in the opposite direction. I felt bewildered and helpless. What was happening to me?

My first couple of days at the Promis Centre were almost blotted out. Physically I felt bruised and aching, as though I'd been beaten up. I was terrified of the smallest thing and unable to function, as if there was a wire in my head that had snapped in two and left me helpless. Though I hadn't admitted it to anyone, I was afraid I might have inherited schizophrenia from my grandmother. But the therapists at the clinic reassured me that I hadn't. They confirmed what

Nick had told me all along, that I was an addict. They also said that addicts often suffer from anxiety and depression, and that all my symptoms were the result of coming off drugs without any kind of support. Addicts need to replace whatever they are addicted to with a structured system of support from other people—either in therapy or through a network—otherwise withdrawal creates such extreme anxiety that it can become overwhelming.

Nick had done his best to communicate this to me, and now trained psychotherapists and psychiatrists were telling me again, but I still didn't get it. I understood that I had a problem. But I thought I'd have the treatment and then be able to go back out and lead a normal life. What I didn't understand was what support really meant, and that it was for the long term. In my head I was saying, *Yeah, right, so sort me out and I'll be on my way.* I still wasn't ready to take the really hard step of admitting responsibility for myself and the choices I'd made. Nor was I yet able to make the link that admitting responsibility was what I needed to do to stay clear of drugs permanently, and to feel sane. I think I found it too hard and too frightening to contemplate a life in which I would need to be in counselling or a Twelve Step group on a weekly, if not daily, basis indefinitely.

As it was, I spent a week in the treatment centre and it certainly did help. The calm environment and daily group therapy brought me back from feeling crazy to feeling I could cope with life again. But even in the centre there were problems. One of the members of my therapy group was still using drugs, and I felt furious that he was getting his stay in the centre paid for by a drug charity and abusing that privilege, while I was paying to be there. So I reported him to the staff. In revenge he told the press that I was there, and gave them all kinds of details about my stay.

I didn't see the papers, as I wasn't going outside the centre and they weren't brought in, but the head counsellor came to me and said the story was in all the tabloids. The whole world was being told that I'd had a breakdown and was suffering from depression after being addicted to drugs. As if that wasn't bad enough, the stories were embellished with lurid and untrue accounts of patients at the Promis Centre walking around in black gowns and being involved in all kinds of weird and wacky treatments. Once I knew that, I felt I couldn't stay. I'd already been finding it hard going, but knowing that several dozen photographers were camped outside the gates watching my every move was too much for me. The staff were kind and supportive, but I felt too exposed and was also very anxious about what my family and my bosses at the BBC would think.

My stepfather, Ted, came to fetch me. I hid in the back of the car and he drove me to his caravan in another part of Kent, where Mum was waiting for me. I wondered how she would feel, now that my drinking and using was out in the open. Would she be angry that I'd kept it hidden from her for so long?

I needn't have worried. Mum gave me a hug and said she was just glad that I was getting help. 'I suspected many times that you were taking drugs,' she said. 'But I never caught you doing it and I suppose I found it easier to look away, because I couldn't have stopped you.' She helped me to laugh about the press. 'Forget what they're saying,' she said. 'You're doing really well, Julie. You've just got to keep going.' I knew she was right. But what I didn't know was whether I was strong enough to do it.

12

CRAZY TIMES

A few days later I went back to work. But, not surprisingly after so brief a stay at the clinic, I still didn't feel really well again. And I was worried about what the rest of the cast would think. It was Sid who broke the ice. He made me laugh, teasing me about all the stuff in the papers. 'They'll have you into black magic and voodoo next,' he joked. 'The wicked witch of *EastEnders*!'

I had only been back at work for a couple of weeks when Jane Harris once again called me into her office. 'I'm worried about you,' she said. 'I can see you're still not well, and I think you need a break. Take a month off and have a proper holiday. We'll miss you, and we'll be waiting for you when you get back.'

What a sensitive approach. She could see I wasn't ready to work again, but knew too that I'd be afraid they didn't want me back. Relieved, I agreed to take a break and wondered what to do. 'I've got some time off too,' Martine said to me. 'How about a holiday together?'

It seemed like a great idea. She'd broken up with

her boyfriend and I'd broken up with mine, so we packed our bags and headed out to Spain for a fortnight. Nellee Hooper, the record producer, had told Martine about a fantastic place just outside Marbella and we booked into a really beautiful hotel where we met two guys called George and Matt. There was no romance—in fact we reckoned they were gay—but they were lovely to us and took us out to dinner. One of them worked for a well-known watch company, and gave us one each. We stayed away from clubs because I didn't want to go near any drink or drugs, and Martine didn't do those things anyway. In fact she was such a hopeless drinker that she got tipsy on a single glass of wine, so mostly she stayed away from the stuff.

She was very patient with me. We'd go out to a restaurant, and then I'd have a panic attack and we'd have to leave. Martine would take control and look after me. I'm sure the people who recognized us had no idea that Tiff and Bianca were on holiday because she was recovering from a broken heart and I was a recovering addict. Or that we were leaving the restaurant because Bianca had had a funny turn. They probably just thought we were being snobbish and walking out.

One day in the town we bumped into Noel and Liam Gallagher, who were with Noel's wife Meg, Kate Moss, actor Johnny Lee Miller and Nellee who had a house there. We were invited over and it was great to be with a crowd of fun and interesting people. I knew Kate from past times when we'd met in clubs, and we chatted for hours. But they were all drinking and I was longing to join in. It was desperately hard staying sober and saying no time after time.

After Nellee's house we went back to the yacht where the others were staying, and continued to party. Everyone was merry, messing about and laughing and joking. It grew chilly and Kate came out on deck with a duvet wrapped round her. I told her about my battle not to drink, and she listened and asked questions. I was pretending to feel fine about it, even though I didn't at all. I managed, however, and at the end of the evening Martine and I went back to our hotel.

I hoped my craving for a drink or some drugs would pass. Surely I deserved that, because I'd been so good and said no? But the next day the craving was still there, and in fact it was getting worse. I felt like someone clinging on to the edge of a cliff, feeling the ground slowly giving way beneath their fingers. Everywhere I looked there were people drinking and having fun, but I was miserable.

That evening Martine and I went out to a trendy bar, packed with well-known faces. We got talking to James Hewitt, the ex-army officer who had taught Princes William and Harry to ride and who, as the world later learned, had a long affair with Princess Diana. From the start it was obvious that he fancied Martine, and though I don't think she was interested in him she enjoyed talking to him and accepted a drink.

Meanwhile I had spotted my hairdresser James Galvin across the bar. He joined us and we chatted for a while, until I saw some other friends of mine, people I knew would almost certainly have drugs on them. I left Martine happily chatting to the two Jameses and went over to my friends. I had been sober and drug-free for almost a year, and for every minute of that year I had felt the most overpowering anxiety. It had been a huge and painful struggle. One of my friends offered me some coke, and at that point my willpower dissolved. I accepted, and headed for the loos to take it. I followed it up with some Ecstasy and a few glasses of champagne. Within minutes all the anxiety drained away and all I could think was, *Why did I leave it so long? Why didn't I have a drink last night? I could have had a laugh, instead of feeling like a taut wire.*

We went on to a seedy club where I carried on drinking until the early hours. Then suddenly someone said, 'Have you heard about Diana and Dodi? They've had a car crash.' I thought it was a joke—albeit a sick one—and I was waiting for the punchline. Then I looked up at the TV behind the bar and realized it was true. At that point the effects of the drugs took a horrible turn: I felt very strange and scared. I knocked back a few brandies to take the edge off the news and made my way back to the hotel in a daze. Like millions of others around the world I found it impossible to take in the idea that Diana, so beautiful and so young, was dead.

There was a personal link for me, too. Two weeks later I had been due to meet her at an AIDS Foundation dinner. I'd met her hairdresser, Sam McKnight, when he did my hair for a *Vogue* photo shoot and he'd told me Diana was a huge fan. Sam said she never missed the Sunday omnibus of *EastEnders* and that she could do a brilliant impression of me as Bianca. He got the photographer on the shoot to do a Polaroid photo of the two of us and asked me to sign it for her, which I did. I'd been so looking forward to meeting her. Now she was dead, and I just couldn't believe it.

Back at the hotel I opened the door to our room to find Martine crying. I began sobbing too, and fell into her arms. Both of us were grieving for Diana, but I was also crying with shame and regret that I'd taken drugs and alcohol. I confessed to Martine what I'd done and she was lovely, comforting me and pointing out that it was a good thing because it reminded me that drugs weren't the answer. That was true. The drugs may have eased my anxiety, but it had been replaced by guilt and a huge sense of failure. Martine said she was sure I would never do it again. I so wanted her to be right, but I wasn't certain I had the faith in myself that she had.

Neither Martine nor I could get over the fact that we'd been with James Hewitt that evening— what a bizarre coincidence. Martine had left him before the news of Diana's death was announced, so we had no idea how he'd reacted, but we were sure that, cad or no cad, he must have been desperately upset.

A couple of days later we flew home. I hadn't taken drugs or a drink again and was feeling a little better, though still very shaken by my relapse. There was another week to go before my month was up and I returned to work, and I was determined to stay clean and put my demons behind me. On the day of Princess Diana's funeral I felt so upset that I went down to Great Ormond Street Hospital, where she had been so often, and asked if there was anything I could do to help. They suggested I went to visit the children on the

197

wards. The nurses told me that many of the kids were terribly sad, so I went and chatted to them and tried to make them laugh. I was so glad to be able to cheer them up a little.

At this time I was at the height of my fame. Everywhere I went I was imitated, swamped by fans and besieged by people shouting, 'Rickaaaaay!' I was asked to do magazine shoots and interviews all the time, and the press leaped on my every move.

Princess Diana hadn't been my only celebrity fan. A few months earlier I had received a call from Tara Palmer-Tomkinson, who was a friend of the royal family, to say that Princes Wills and Harry were fans and could Wills (then aged fourteen) have a photo of me naked to put on his bedroom wall at Eton? I was scandalized and thought, *Wait till I meet their mum—I'll tell her*! But of course I never got the chance. Then the brother of a friend of mine worked on an ad with Madonna, who had her hair dyed red for it. He told me that she spent most of the day parodying Bianca and yelling, 'Rickaaaaay!', much to the amusement of the film crew. And Julie Walters—one of the best actresses in Britain and someone I respect and admire tremendously—asked me for my autograph for her daughter. Later she sent me a beautiful letter telling me that I had so many of the same qualities that she'd had as a young actress and that she could see a lot of herself in me. I was so happy when I read those words that I screamed. It made everything I'd ever gone through seem worthwhile, and I am eternally grateful to Julie. I still have the letter, and whenever I doubt myself, as I often do, I remind myself of what she said.

I was often parodied on TV too—Bianca's

famous tacky silver jacket became her trademark, and impersonators loved it. And even the Queen appeared to be a fan. She came to visit the *EastEnders* set and seemed to be familiar with all the characters, chatting happily with us as if she knew us. But while I revelled in the compliments and tributes and loved my public life, privately I was still struggling. After coming back from holiday I went into aftercare for a month. Promis had a place in Knightsbridge in central London where I could go during the day for meetings and support; I went several times a week, and it helped. I managed to stay off drink and drugs, but I was still getting panic attacks and feeling very unwell.

Since the split from Nick I had really missed him. So I was very happy when, not long after my return from holiday, he got in touch to say he had missed me too and wanted to try again. I was sure that being with Nick was the key to solving all my problems, and this time he agreed to move in with Charley and me and make a real go of family life. At last I'd got what I wanted—Nick was back, and he was living with us. So why wasn't I as happy as I thought I'd be? I was sure everything would be perfect, but it wasn't. Although the two men in my life had a lovely relationship and Nick always made time to play with Charley, I felt my partner wasn't always there for me. Nick worked long hours because his career was taking off, and I felt he was obsessed with work. He was writing a script for a film called *Football Factory*, as well as making other films, and it felt to me as though his work was his first priority.

Looking back, I can see that I was selfish and that neither of us was ready to put in the time and effort it takes to make a relationship work. So much of the time, Nick and I wanted different things. I was ready for family life; a friend of mine used to call it 'white picket fence syndrome', and although I didn't get it at the time I can now see exactly what she meant. I wanted the perfect family and home, picket fence and all. Meanwhile Nick was passionate about his career. And on top of these differences, I was still in denial about my drinking and drug-taking.

He would often tell me, 'You're a raging addict, and you need to go and sort it out', but I had no idea what he meant. After all, I wasn't using, I wasn't on a park bench somewhere—so what was the problem? I'd proved that I could stop, so that meant I wasn't an addict, right? Wrong, on all counts. I didn't understand then that addiction, or alcoholism, is an illness that never goes away. Stopping the drink and drugs doesn't mean you're no longer an addict. The cravings, anxiety and depression are still there, and the only way to deal with them is to get support.

It's how you know you're an addict or an alcoholic. While some people can drink or take drugs and then just decide to stop and be fine, for addicts it's not that simple. They have to make a conscious decision, every day, to remain clean and sober, or it's all too easy to plunge back into the craziness. And to make that daily choice, they need support. This can take various forms, but for some addicts what works best is the Twelve Step Programme—with which I'd already made slight aquaintance—because it provides such a clear structure and support network.

All this was still a long way off for me, though. I

was going through my daily battle alone, and as a result suffering anxiety and depression. But I was blind to what was happening, so I kept resorting to new solutions which I was sure would sort my life out. It wasn't enough for Nick to have moved in, I decided; we needed to be married. Then everything would be all right. Nick didn't really want to get married. But he loved me and he went along with the plan, perhaps hoping that it really would make me happy and give us more stability.

We got married in August 1998. We'd wanted to do so in Spain, but that proved complicated. Most of the churches there are Catholic, and although I had been baptized into the Catholic Church because of my father's family, Nick hadn't, and he wouldn't have been allowed to marry there. So we decided to have two weddings—a low-key official one in London followed by a blessing and a big family party in Spain.

The first was in Bow Town Hall, where we had planned a quickie ceremony with a couple of friends as witnesses. After organizing heavy security outside so that the press couldn't take pictures, we went in hidden behind umbrellas. But disaster then struck when we discovered that the bookings had somehow got muddled and we weren't due to be there until the next day. Trouble was, the next day we were flying out to Spain with all our family and friends for the real celebrations. In the end we had to let our fifty or so guests go to Spain ahead of us, while we went back to the town hall. Then we followed them out to La Manga, a place we had been to on holiday and loved.

OK magazine had bought the rights to the wedding pictures in Spain. We agreed to the deal because the fee they paid covered the cost of flying everyone out there business class, plus their hotel rooms. It was a fairytale day. I wore a stunning dress of antique lace in gold and cream. It fitted like a glove, all the way from the corset top to the fishtail train, which was held by my little bridesmaids who looked like fairies. My old friend Nicole was chief bridesmaid and she looked lovely. Six-year-old Charley wore a little Armani suit, with larger ones for Nick and his friend Charles, who was best man. Among our friends who came to wish us well were Sid, Martine and Richard Driscoll, who played the on/off part of the priest in *EastEnders*.

At the reception afterwards everyone was having a great time except me. Most people were drinking, and once again I wanted to—so badly that I couldn't enjoy myself or think about anything else. I was trying to please everyone and do the right thing, but I was miserable because my craving overwhelmed any other feeling. It was a sad way to be on my wedding day, but I didn't know at that time that there was any other way. I was staying away from drink and drugs, for Nick's sake and for my own, in the only way I knew how. We stayed in Spain for several more days and I went through the motions of enjoying myself. But inside I was thinking, *Why aren't I happy now? I've got what I wanted, so why doesn't everything feel perfect?*

Back home I threw myself into work. *EastEnders* was as demanding as ever, and I also agreed to be in a short film that Nick was making called *Love Story*. I played a pregnant heroin addict—how many times was it that I had played an addict?— and loved the role because there were some brilliant actors appearing alongside me. David Thewlis, Jamie Forman and Paul Nichols—who had recently been in *EastEnders*—were all in the cast, and my brother Harry had a small part too. The film was to appear on the end of the DVD for Nick's longer film, *Football Factory*, which was about football hooligans. Despite the great cast it wasn't easy working with Nick. We are both strong characters, and I found to hard to take direction from him without arguing and making my own suggestions. But we managed, and in the end it was a good little film.

Over the next few months our relationship limped along, but things weren't good because of my constant anxiety and depression. It was a strange, sad time. On the surface everything was perfect and no one would have guessed how miserable I felt. I was a hot actress, Nick was a hot young director, and together we were a hot couple, as they put it in those days. I was winning awards from magazines like *TV Quick*, *Inside Soap* and *Smash Hits*, and I was voted Best Actress in the *Elle* Style Awards. Everyone wanted to be seen with us, and Nick and I were asked to trendy parties and premieres and given all kinds of wonderful freebies.

Vespa, for instance, gave me a beautiful scooter, cream-coloured with brown leather seats. Sid Owen got one too, and both he and I went and took our motorcycle tests so that we could ride them. The whole story was in *OK* magazine and I remember riding back home from my test, petrified but trying not to show it, looking like Lady Penelope from *Thunderbirds* in my white helmet and scarf and sunglasses. Most of the time Nick rode the Vespa, with me perched on the pillion. But eventually I got fed up with it and, since I had been asked to be patron of an AIDS charity for children, I gave it to them to auction to raise funds.

By this time I'd realized that fame could be a real help in giving charities a profile, and I was glad to do what I could. But for a long time I'd been so insecure that I was embarrassed and convinced I couldn't do much. Once I got past that stage and understood that I really could be of some use I enjoyed the work a lot. I became patron of a couple of children's charities—small ones that didn't have any government assistance and often struggled to keep going. Whenever I saw kids who were ill or homeless or hungry, I wondered why some of us have so much and some so little. I felt passionately about my charity work and wanted to save the world. Later I became involved with the National Society for the Prevention of Cruelty to Children (NSPCC) and met Prince Andrew, the charity's patron, a number of times. He was always very relaxed, charming and humorous.

Fictional children were in my life at this time, too. In *EastEnders*, Bianca was pregnant. I had to get used to strapping on padding for the screen, so I was relieved when her son Liam was born on Christmas Day 1998. Typically for Bianca, there was high drama and the birth took place in the Queen Vic pub!

Happy with a child at last, Bianca and Ricky were perfect for one another—anyone could see that. But while my on-screen persona had the right man, I began to be convinced that in real life I didn't. Four months into our marriage, Sid and I were invited on a cruise around the coast of

Portugal and Spain. We and our partners would get a free holiday in exchange for us two EastEnders giving a talk to the passengers. Sid brought his brother Darren and a couple of friends, and I took Charley and Nick.

From the start Nick and I didn't get on well. He would rather not have been on the cruise and I was craving drugs, so we were constantly bickering and snapping at one another. After a couple of days we hit bad weather and I started to feel very ill. I took some anti-seasickness tablets, which helped—and I noticed that they were giving me a bit of a buzz. I liked the feeling, which reminded me of the high that drugs had given me, so I took more and more of the tablets—first three, then five, and then ten at a time. Soon I was out of it and no longer able to control what I was doing. I headed for the bar and ordered myself a drink. Nick was worried, but all I could think was, *I'll show you—I can have a drink if I want one.* Of course, it wasn't just one drink; one would never be enough. I had several, and ended up staggering around the bar. Two years of staying clean and sober went out of the window. Nick walked off and left me to it: he felt deeply disappointed, let down and tired of the way I was behaving.

We managed to get through the rest of the cruise somehow and were both relieved to be home again. From that point I didn't even try to stay sober or clean, but began drinking regularly again and went back to using cocaine. I told myself I didn't care, I loved being high—it felt better than being anxious and unhappy. I went out with my mates until three or four in the morning, binge-drinking and taking huge amounts of drugs. I decided I was bored with the life that Nick and I had. All he did was work—or at least that's how it seemed to me—and I wanted to have fun. *There's more to life than work*, I told myself. *My mates are a lot more fun than Nick is—they know how to enjoy themselves*. And of course they did, if your idea of enjoying yourself is to get totally smashed. I was back hanging out with the kind of people who'd join me in drink and drug binges and do what I wanted, instead of disapproving, trying to get me to stop and refusing to join me.

Less than a month after the cruise I asked Nick to leave. I told him we weren't compatible and I'd fallen out of love. And I told him it was his fault, for working too hard. He must have been very hurt. He'd been unsure about marrying me in the first place, and he'd been right. But while I blotted everything out with drink and drugs and blamed him for not giving me what I wanted, Nick didn't blame me: he accepted that the marriage was over and moved out. I know I behaved badly. But we both also knew that ending the marriage was for the best, however messily it was done. Nick was a lovely man and we had each convinced ourselves we were right for each other. In fact I was so sure for so long that I ignored the obvious—something was always missing between us. We had surface chemistry, but we were never going to have the deep connection you need with another person to make a marriage work.

13

A BEGINNING AND AN ENDING

When Nick left I decided I wanted to be young, free and single again. I went to loads of parties to make up for lost time, and my drinking and drug-taking became worse than ever. No doubt I was blotting out the guilt I felt at hurting not only Nick but Charley too. My son had been close to Nick and now really missed him. But I persuaded myself that these things were short-term and I was only seeing myself through the pain of the break-up. I always had an excuse.

One morning a week or two after Nick departed, coming back down to earth after a chemically induced high I realized with horror what an idiot I was being. I panicked at how much hurt I'd caused, so I rang Nick and did my best to get him to come back. He said no, and I'm glad he did. It was a knee-jerk reaction on my part and would only have led to an even bigger mess. In fact Nick and I didn't see one another again for a long time. I set the divorce in motion straightaway, and Nick agreed that I could sue him on grounds of unreasonable behaviour and he wouldn't contest it. This was generous of him, as my behaviour had been far more unreasonable than his. I'm glad to say that Nick and I did become friends, eventually. We both know that life's too short to hang on to old hurts.

Meanwhile Mum and Ted took Charley on holiday with them and a friend of mine, Jo, moved in with me. We'd been good friends since I'd been in my tiny flat and her boyfriend had lived next door. She had just split up with him and had been staying with her mum, so she was glad of a place to go and I was grateful for the company.

While Charley was away Jo and I decided to go to a health farm called Henlow Grange for a few days. I wanted some space to get over the end of my marriage and to detox without temptations all around me. We had a terrific few days there, and towards the end of our stay who should turn up but Sid. He was about to go skiing and asked me if I'd like to go along. I would be back before Charley came home and so, revelling in being able to do what I wanted without having to ask anyone else, I decided to go.

Sid and I set off for Switzerland with my friend Nicole and her new boyfriend, Daniel. On the plane I got stuck into the brandy, and by the time we landed I'd got through most of a bottle. We arrived in the evening and, already drunk, I headed straight for the bar, where I bumped into a group of friends from back home. They gave me some cocaine, which I sniffed in the loo, before partying for most of the night. By ten the next morning, when the others were setting off for a day's skiing, I was lying in my chalet wanting to die. I felt ill, hungover and ashamed. I was so frightened that the press might see me that I locked the door and refused to come out. Once again I promised myself I'd never do it again. Luckily, by the next day I was feeling better and was able to join the others on the slopes for the remaining four days of our trip.

We got home a couple of days before Charley was due back. Knowing how tough the split with Nick had been for him, I'd arranged to buy him a puppy in the hope that it would cheer him up. Nicole came with me to collect her, a tiny, wrinkly Shar-pei we called Leila. When Mum brought Charley to the house after their holiday I put Leila in the middle of the floor so that he'd see her as soon as he walked in. His face lit up. He fell in love with her, as I had. She was to become a much-loved member of our family.

A few days later I was round at Mum's, sitting in the kitchen having a cup of tea with her and Harry, who'd dropped in too. We were chatting about mutual friends when Harry suddenly asked, 'Would you ever go out on a date with Richie?'

'He'd never go out with me,' I replied, but Harry insisted, 'He would, you know.'

I didn't think much more about it. Richie was great—I'd fancied him since I was a gawky kid of eleven and he was my big brother's gorgeous friend, far too grown up at nineteen to think of me as more than a kid. Over the years we'd met many times and become friends—I'd even spent the night on his sofa once, after a party. That time things had changed between us and we'd almost had a kiss— but true to form I'd been sick, so nothing had happened. Richie had just tucked me up on the sofa and the next day I'd thought, *Forget it—it was just a drunken moment and he doesn't really fancy me.*

Now here was Harry suggesting that perhaps Richie did fancy me after all. I hoped it was true— but how was I to know? And in any case, here I was fresh out of a disastrous marriage, and as far as I knew Richie had a girlfriend and had been with her for three years.

A week later it was Valentine's Day. I had to go

to a ball for a children's leukaemia charity, but Jo asked me if I wanted to join her and some friends at the Emporium nightclub afterwards. She was going with a guy called Tony, whom she'd just begun dating. 'He's bringing his friend, Richie Merkell,' she said. 'He's just split up with his girlfriend.' Suddenly here I was, on Valentine's Day, about to get together with Richie and—best of all—he was single again. It sounded too good to be true.

That night both Richie and I knew that something had changed between us. After all the years of friendship, we both felt ready for a real relationship. We laughed and danced, and as we stood talking at the bar he leaned over and kissed me. It was so unexpected, and so good. Richie told me I looked lovely, and I felt it. I hoped this would be the start of something wonderful—but then I ruined it. I didn't take any drugs that night, but I had several glasses of wine and got very tipsy. We all went back to my house, where—no surprise—I was sick all over the place. My romantic night ended with Richie, Tony and Jo putting me to bed and cleaning up. Richie slept on the sofa.

I had to be up early the next morning because I was due to film an episode of Michael Barrymore's show *Kids Say the Funniest Things*. Charley loved the programme, so I was doing it for him. By the time I'd got up, early though it was, Richie was already leaving for work. I was sure he wouldn't be interested in me any longer. I'd been given my chance to be a gorgeous seductress, to show him how adult I was—and what did I do? Throw up. I cringed just at the memory of it, and was convinced I'd ruined everything.

I wondered whether he would ever call me, or even speak to me, again. But the next day he phoned, laughing, to ask how I was. When I apologized for being sick he told me not to worry and asked me out to dinner. On the evening he suggested, a couple of nights later, I had been invited by Prince Andrew to St James's Palace for an NSPCC do. I told Richie it wouldn't last long and that, if he waited outside the palace in his black cab once he'd finished work, I'd meet him there and we could go for something to eat.

I had been very flattered to be asked to the palace. I wasn't sure quite what kind of do it was, but imagined there would be lots of celebrities milling around. I didn't know Prince Andrew well, though we'd met a number of times through the charity. We'd had our photo taken together not long before, with Charley sitting between us in what looked like a font. I've no idea why the photographer used a font—I think it was just a way of posing us as if we were a couple with our small child. I understood what he was getting at when I saw it in *Hello*; Mum and I ended up crying with laughter because with my red hair I looked ridiculously like Fergie, the Prince's ex-wife.

That evening I turned up at the palace to find that I was the only well-known face there. Apart from the Prince and myself there were some NSPCC officials—and that was it. I'd imagined that I could blend into the background and then slip out, but instead the whole focus was on me. I had no idea why—it did cross my mind that the Prince might fancy me, but I soon dismissed the thought. I'm sure I talked far too much and probably drove him mad!

211

The Prince was charming, showing me round the palace, offering me champagne and being very witty and amusing. We had a very pleasant couple of hours, but I could barely concentrate. I knew Richie would be waiting outside, and when the time for our date approached I gulped the last of my champagne, told Prince Andrew, 'Sorry, but I've got to go', and raced outside.

I jumped into the back of Richie's waiting taxi, giggling about how mad it all seemed. We then had a wonderful evening, sitting and talking and laughing and looking into one another's eyes. The energy between us was electric, and it felt different from anything I had ever experienced before. I felt I had grown up at last. I wasn't the silly little girl he'd first met but a woman of twenty-six, with a son and a home of my own and a great job. And he was thirty-four, a man and not a boy, hard-working, clear about what he wanted and strong enough to be himself no matter what happened. He was also not in the least over-awed because my face was well known—he'd known me too long for that.

I knew something special had begun. But was this the right moment for it? Richie was incredibly close to his family, and had been devastated when his father had been diagnosed with cancer a few months earlier. He told me he'd given up his flat and moved back home to help his parents, and so I wasn't sure whether he would have much time for a new romance. Luckily for me, he felt as strongly as I did and there was no question about us not being together. After that first date we saw each other almost every day, and within a few weeks Richie had moved in with me and Charley.

I was still drinking and taking drugs, but because

I was so happy with Richie I found I was doing it far less. I just didn't seem to crave them in the same way—it was as though I was on a natural high and didn't need the false one as much. Richie helped me, too. He liked a drink but he knew when to stop, and if he saw me carrying on too long he'd just take me home. And I didn't protest, because I didn't want to stay on without him.

Richie's attitude to my drinking and using was very calm and accepting. He didn't make any dramas, give me any ultimatums or tell me what to do. He made it clear that he loved me no matter what I did, and would always be there for me. He was offering me the security I had always longed for. But if I felt that because of this new dimension in my life my habit didn't rule me any more I was lying to myself, because although I was using and drinking less I couldn't actually control my habit. There were still times when I got off my head, and in April 1999 I let down a good friend because I went out and got totally wasted.

Barbara Windsor and I had become real pals off the set at *EastEnders*. We hardly ever had scenes together, but we'd sit and chat while we were both waiting to go on. When she was invited to attend a Variety Club of Great Britain lunch at the Dorchester to receive one of their Silver Hearts for her outstanding contribution to showbusiness, she invited me to come too and even arranged for me to sit next to her during the meal. I was thrilled, and promised to be there. It would be a huge event with dozens of stars, and Barbara was to be paid tributes by Jim Davidson, Dale Winton and Paul Daniels.

It really mattered to me to be there for her. So

what did I do? I partied with some mates the night before and went completely wild. Why I did it the night before something so important I don't know, except that I was always capable of pressing a huge self-destruct button. Richie was working, so there was no one to stop me, and I simply didn't have the willpower to stop myself. I took so many little pills and drank so much that the next day I couldn't move. I rang the studies and lied to Barbara about being ill, then lay in bed throwing up and crying because I had let myself and everyone else down so badly. When I got into work the following day I went to find Barbara to apologize. She was sitting in make-up and looked more angry than I had ever seen her. Almost believing my own lie, I repeated that I had been unwell and said sorry. Barbara, knowing full well that I was lying, told me to fuck off.

I couldn't believe it. I knew she was right, but few people had ever been so direct or so angry with me and I was shocked. I shouted at her and she shouted back. Full of pride and guilt, I stormed off. Having barely ever appeared together before, it seemed for the next few weeks as though Peggy and Bianca were together in almost all our scenes. Barbara and I would do the scene together with total professionalism—we'd never have let our dispute get in the way of the job. But after we'd finished we'd stalk off in opposite directions, ignoring one another—two East End girls acting like raging hotheads. This went on for a couple of months, until we were both nominated for Best Actress in the British Soap Awards. Barbara won, and we were able to rekindle our friendship over a few glasses of champagne and even to have a cuddle.

I had huge respect for Barbara. She, more than anyone, understood me. Although she hadn't been through addiction she had so much life experience that there wasn't much she didn't understand. June Brown, who plays Dot Cotton, was another wise woman and a great friend. I loved listening to the magical stories she told with such amazing detail. She was also very funny and had astonishing energy. We younger cast members might complain of being tired, but she never ever did—though to be fair she did say she used to be more tired when she was in her twenties and holding down a job while bringing up her children. She told Charley and me that when her children were small they slept in her dressing room while she was on stage, and she would check on them in the intervals. During the two and a half years I spent in the theatre after I left *EastEnders* I thought often of June, as I took my own two small children with me and let them sleep in the dressing room just as she had described. There was something magical about working on stage with my children just yards away fast asleep—it felt very wholesome and real.

For the next few months I worked hard at *EastEnders*, Richie worked hard driving his cab, and we both loved and looked after Charley, who accepted Richie from the start. And of course Richie also spent a lot of time with his parents, doing all he could to support his dad and help his mum. There was only one problem, and that was my relationship with my own mum. We had always been incredibly close and she had supported me through so much, but she was shocked that my marriage had come and gone so fast and that I was

215

already seeing someone else. It wasn't that she didn't like Richie—she had known him for twenty years as Harry's friend and had always liked him. But she thought it was much too soon for me to be in a new relationship, and she wasn't convinced that Richie was the right man for me.

What she felt was not unreasonable, but I just wasn't willing to see it. I was certain that Richie was right for me, and very resentful that Mum wouldn't accept the way I felt. We didn't have blazing rows, more a series of short, blunt exchanges over a period of weeks as my resentment built up. I convinced myself that Mum had babied me for too long, and that I needed to break free of her and of our deeply enmeshed relationship in order to be myself and make my own decisions. I was angry that she hadn't given my relationship with Richie more of a chance before deciding he wasn't right for me. And whereas in the past I had almost always taken Mum's advice and felt that she knew best, I decided it was time I did things my own way. I had been too dependent on her, and now I needed to think for myself.

A lot of this was deeply unfair to Mum, but I couldn't see that at all. A huge well of resentment had built up within me—as so often with drug addiction—and it was all pouring out. I told her not to interfere in my life, and a distance grew between us. We still saw each other, but less often, and things were strained. The easy companionship was gone.

Other changes were in the air too. After a lot of thought I had decided to leave *EastEnders*. There were a number of things that prompted the decision. First, I had been working very hard on the series for six years and was simply tired of the constant pressure. Then, a few weeks earlier, I had had to miss Charley's sports day because I was filming. It really upset me, because previously I'd always managed to be at his school for all the important events. I didn't want my job to be more important than my son. And when I got together with Richie and we began talking about marriage and having children together, I realized that I wanted to make changes and to be able to spend more time with him and with Charley. I also wanted the opportunity to spread my wings a little and try other things, on stage as well as on television. I'd grown in confidence as an actress and I longed to play other roles, just to discover my full potential.

I knew there was no guarantee of work—many ex-*EastEnders* actors have disappeared into obscurity. But I was willing to take the chance. I had saved up enough money to be able to manage without an income for a while, and it was the right time to go because my popularity was at a peak.

But equally, that popularity made it very hard to walk away. In the year I left I won a number of awards. I was voted Best Actress in the *Smash Hits* Poll of 1999, I won Most Stylish Female in the *Elle* magazine awards and, best of all, I received a nomination in the British Soap Awards which were to be held in 2000. At this time my face was on so many magazine covers that I didn't even notice them any more—I'd go round the supermarket doing my shopping and barely give them a second glance. It wasn't that I was arrogant, just that I was in them so often I couldn't have kept up even if I'd wanted to. At one point I was in *OK* magazine every week for several months. I also received huge numbers of invitations to all kinds of functions. One of the grandest was when Michael Winner invited me to director Stanley Kubrick's memorial dinner and I sat on a table with Maureen Lipman, Joanna Lumley and Alan Parker, hardly able to believe that I was in such exalted company.

I enjoyed the fame and felt very lucky. Bianca had just taken off as a character, and I had always had a huge amount of press interest and attention. I'd learned to manage it and had moved on from Anna Scher to a bigger agent, ICM, one of the largest and most successful in the world of showbiz. But what I felt I really wanted now was to have a break for a few months, just to rest and enjoy being with Richie and Charley, and then to go on to other work. So I plucked up my courage and went to see the producers.

They weren't happy that I was leaving, and told me that Bianca was one of the show's best characters. They asked for time to write her out, and we agreed, very amicably, that I would stay on for six months. They were also generous enough to say that the door would be left open for me to return, and that they hoped I would stay with the BBC and do other programmes. I would love to, I told them—after I'd had a break.

Just before I left I was invited to a meeting with several heads of BBC departments, including drama, drama serial and film. Mum and my agent came with me. I was told that they wanted to keep me at the BBC and hoped I'd have a long career with them; they described me as one of Britain's best-loved actresses, and asked me what I wanted to do. There was some discussion about developing a number of projects specifically for me. As at the meeting with the *EastEnders* producers, I thanked them and said I'd like to take a break and then I'd be happy to consider a new project. I left feeling that everything looked very rosy.

All sorts of exciting possibilities were suggested in due course. At one point I was asked to come in to the BBC to meet an exciting young actor called Orlando Bloom. They were developing a possible series about a judge's son and a gangster's daughter, and wanted to cast the two of us. 'He's really going to be hot stuff,' they told me, and since I was considered hot stuff too they reckoned it would be a surefire success. When I met Orlando, who was then just twenty-two, five years younger than me, he was very nervous but couldn't have been nicer to me. 'I can't believe I've met you!' he said. 'I'm your biggest fan.' We got on really well, but for some reason—I've never known why—nothing further came of the project.

I was also contacted by the actor Charles Dance, who had been trying to get the rights to Shaw's play *Pygmalion* (better known to many people in its musical version, *My Fair Lady*) so that he could film an adaptation for the BBC, with himself as Professor Higgins and me as Eliza Doolittle. I loved the idea; I had always liked period dramas, though the only one I'd been in so far was *Clarissa*, which starred Sean Bean. I was pregnant with Charley at the time and kept falling asleep! The Charles Dance production sounded perfect, but sadly, like a lot of great TV ideas, it never came to fruition. Not long afterwards Trevor Nunn put on *My Fair Lady* in the West End with Martine McCutcheon in the role of Eliza. The press claimed at the time that I'd auditioned for it, but that wasn't true—it was the Charles Dance project that I'd been involved in.

In my last few weeks on *EastEnders* Bianca's final storyline found her having an affair with her mother Carol's boyfriend Dan, played by Craig Fairbrass. Dan had been Bianca's older boyfriend before she moved to the Square, and when her mum introduced him as her new man it wasn't long before he and Bianca rekindled their affair. They called it off when they discovered that Carol was pregnant by Dan, and Bianca and Ricky made plans to move to Manchester so that Bianca could attend fashion college there. However, Carol found out about the affair and so did Ricky. Devastated, the two of them told Bianca they wanted nothing more to do with her, and she left for Manchester to begin a new life with her son Liam.

On my last day on the show, in August 1999, I couldn't stop crying because I felt so sad to be leaving them all. Lindsay Coulson, my screen mum, presented me with a collage of photos of all the members of the cast and crew, and many of the others gave me beautiful cards and gifts. My very last scene was shot at night. Richie came with me, to watch, as I filmed Bianca's goodbye to Ricky. It was so emotional that I couldn't look at Sid without crying, but luckily that fitted the storyline. I knew I was going to miss them all so much.

14

A BABY AND A WEDDING

Despite the tearful ending the previous evening, the next morning I woke up feeling excited that I had so many possibilities ahead of me. It felt strange not to be going off to work at Elstree, but I knew I'd soon be working again and in the meantime I was looking forward to some free time. Charley was seven and a half and due to start at a new school in a couple of weeks. Up till now he'd been at a Montessori school near home, where he was very happy, but it only took children up to the age of seven. For the next stage of his education I'd chosen a small private school in Woodford, Essex. It was some distance for us to travel each day, but it was a great school and Richie and I had begun to think about moving out of the East End and closer to the school. Charley and I spent a lovely couple of weeks together before term started, and because I was no longer filming I was able to take him there myself and help him settle in, which meant a lot to me.

I had been told that there were some exciting series in development for me, but these wouldn't be happening for at least a year, which suited me just fine. *McCready and Daughter* was to be a detective series, with actor Toby Doyle and me in the title roles. And *Red Cap* was to be about a girl in the army. I was included in the meetings to help develop the character from scratch, and was thrilled because for me it was something new and different. Meanwhile I planned to take a few months off and then see what came along.

What I didn't bargain for was becoming pregnant. It was a few weeks before Christmas when I made the discovery, so the baby was due the following August. Although it wasn't planned Richie and I had agreed that we wanted children together and we were pleased to bits. I hoped that I'd be able to fit work around it, but whether or not, I knew this baby would come first.

When I went round to tell Mum I was pregnant I hoped that, despite her reservations about Richie and me, she would be happy for me and it would give us an opportunity to heal our differences. So when I saw the disapproving look on her face I felt terribly disappointed. The resentment I had been feeling for months came to a head and we had a huge row. I accused her of not caring about the baby and not wanting me to be happy. Then I walked away, determined to break off contact with her altogether.

It was an insensitive, foolish way to behave. When I stormed off I knew in my heart of hearts that I was wrong to do it, and that she did care. But I was set on a course and there was no going back. I told myself I was going to do things my way and live my own life without my mum breathing down my neck. If I'd known then how much I was going to miss her over the coming months, I'd have turned back. But I convinced myself that she was out of my life and that was it.

Richie just couldn't understand what all the fuss was about. His dad was dying, and compared to that anything else was unimportant. He thought Mum and I should just sit down and sort things out.

But I certainly wasn't ready to do that.

As soon as I knew I was pregnant I stopped drinking and using. I was lucky in that, just as during my first pregnancy, I was able to stop without any noticeable side-effects. Perhaps it was because my body was in hormonal upheaval. But what I also had once again was sickness, all the way through. In fact it turned out to be a very difficult and frightening pregnancy and I did wonder sometimes whether that could have been a result of all my excesses, although the doctors assured me it wasn't.

Not only was I sick a lot, but this time I was also bleeding frequently. I was in and out of hospital on drips, just as before, and felt terrible most of the time. Despite these problems I managed to make a three-part programme about the East End and to present a little series about Battersea Dogs' Home, which I really enjoyed. But once that had been filmed the doctors warned me not to take anything else on until after the birth.

Richie's father Emilio, who was Spanish, had been ill for a long while. He'd kept going far longer than had been predicted, but by February 2000 we knew he was near the end. We often used to go over to see him and sometimes stayed with Emilio and Richie's mum Jackie for a few days. They were a wonderfully warm, close family. Richie's sisters Tessa and Vanessa were both married and Vanessa had two children, Sam and Amy. The whole lot came over to Emilio and Jackie's every week. They all loved home-cooked meals and Jackie was a fantastic cook. One day they asked me if I could cook. 'Oh yes,' I said. I thought cooking was pouring curry sauce out of a tin, and had no idea what real cooking was until they showed me.

Not long before Emilio died I was sitting at the table with him. I was feeling low that day, worrying about the baby and missing my mum. He got up and walked around the table—which was a painstakingly slow, difficult task for him at that stage because he was so ill. He gave me a big hug. 'Don't worry,' he told me. 'I know how you feel, but everything is going to be all right.' What he said that day meant such a lot to me, and I never forgot his kindness. He knew he wouldn't live to see our baby born, but his encouraging words carried me through the next few difficult months.

One day while we were staying with him and Jackie I suddenly had a powerful feeling that I should leave, and that the family should be together on their own. So I went and hugged Emilio, said goodbye and went home with Charley. The next day Emilio died. Richie came home a few hours later, devastated. Despite knowing that this sad event was coming, he just couldn't believe that his father had gone. As he grieved over the next few months, knowing that our baby was coming helped him through. What neither of us knew then was that my pregnancy wasn't just difficult but dangerous. I had a condition which was actually life-threatening for both me and the baby, and would lead to a dramatic and frightening premature birth.

Thank goodness we were ignorant of the drama to come, because the next two or three months were tough enough for us. Richie was grieving for his dad and trying to support his mum, while I continued to feel horribly sick all the time. And although I was far too stubborn to make up with

Mum, I was finding the present state of things hard going without her support.

The one highlight was the British Soap Awards 2000. Although I had left *EastEnders* I had been nominated for Best Actress for my performances the previous year. By the time the ceremony came around I was heavily pregnant and sticking out a mile. I didn't know what on earth to wear so I asked the advice of Richie's sister Vanessa, who worked in a boutique called Shop 77 which boasted quite a few well-known customers including Tara Palmer-Tomkinson, Lisa Snowdon and Victoria Beckham. Vanessa found me a perfect black skirt and top which were comfortable as well as glamorous. I added a pink pashmina and the whole outfit looked great.

As Richie and I posed on the red carpet outside I felt very nervous because I'd been tipped off that I might win—though after my earlier experience with Robbie Williams I wasn't taking any rumours too seriously. That fabulous actor James Fox, one of the English greats, presented the Best Actress category, and I was so stunned when he read out my name as the winner that I almost forgot to go up and receive it. He told me he was a huge fan, which meant almost as much to me as the award itself.

That moment of glory buoyed me up in what was otherwise a tough time. Because of the continued bleeding my consultant obstetrician at the Portland Hospital, a wonderful Egyptian doctor called Mr Hazeem al-Rafeay, decided to send me for a more detailed scan. When he got the results he explained that I had a condition called Vassa Praevia, in which the placenta is divided into two parts connected by a blood vessel. The baby's head was pressing against that blood vessel, which meant that any force or abrupt movement could cause the blood vessel to rupture. No more award ceremonies, work or even shopping trips, Hazeem warned me. The baby would probably have to be delivered early, and I would almost certainly need to spend some time in hospital before the birth. Richie and I were understandably shocked.

Hazeem transferred me at just under six months to the Chelsea and Westminster Hospital, which was better equipped for the specialist care I needed. I must have total rest until the birth, Hazeem told me, which he would try to put off for a month, hoping to get me to thirty-two weeks in order to give the baby the best possible chance. It was a very frightening time. Although I didn't know until later just how bad the odds were, I was well aware that something could easily go wrong and I was terrified of losing the baby.

We knew, from the many scans I'd had, that I was expecting a boy, and we'd already decided to call him Fenton, a name that appealed to us both and also that of a much-loved cousin of mine. Day after day, sitting in hospital, I talked to little Fenton, encouraging him to keep going and to arrive safely in our arms. Richie and Charley moved into the hospital too, so that we were all living there together in a room which had been made into a sort of mini-hotel. Charley was wonderful—he understood how important it was, and made no fuss about having to live away from his home and everyday surroundings. We made the place as friendly and familiar as we could, putting his football posters on the walls and bringing some of his toys over. Richie's sisters were wonderful, too. Vanessa often came and took Charley to school, and he frequently spent time at her or Tessa's home afterwards, playing with their children.

Occasionally Hazeem would allow me out of the hospital to the Italian restaurant across the road. I had to promise not to go further than five minutes away, but that little bit of freedom helped to alleviate the boredom and endless waiting. Sometimes we ventured round to the Bluebird, a pub in the King's Road. Harry came to see us the day before the baby was to be delivered, and the three of us went there for lunch.

By mid-June I'd made it to the vital thirty-two weeks and Hazeem said he didn't want to wait any longer. He told us the birth date would be 13 June. I was very cheerful, relieved that the waiting was coming to an end at last. I had no idea then that the birth itself was also very dangerous and that this was to be far from a normal caesarean. I'm so glad they didn't tell me, because I was tense enough about having the epidural, which I dreaded, without the added anxiety of knowing that my life and that of my baby were hanging in the balance.

I laughed at the sight of Richie in his theatre gown and mask, which he had had to put on so that he could come with us. Hazeem warned me that the caesarean would take longer than usual, but reassured me that I'd be having the best possible care. I trusted him completely and was certain he would make sure we were all right.

The anaesthetist had to make several attempts at inserting the epidural needle because I was so rigid with nerves. He tried to relax me with jokes, asking what music he should put on and suggesting 'The First Cut Is the Deepest'. Once the epidural was in I felt sure the worst was over. Hazeem warned me that although I would feel no pain I'd be aware of things going on inside me, but I couldn't see anything and so I just lay back and waited.

Minutes later my baby was born. Fenton weighed only four pounds three ounces and had to be taken straight to special care. A nurse brought him over to me on the way, a minute bundle with a scrunched up little face, and then he was gone. Richie went with him, and I felt so relieved it was all over that I was on a high and as soon as I was taken to the recovery room I was on my mobile, phoning family and friends to tell them I'd had the baby. Soon after that they put me in a wheelchair and took me round to the special care unit to see Fenton. He looked so vulnerable, lying in his cot all hooked up to wires and drips. I sat beside him and held his tiny hand, full of gratitude that he'd made it.

Much later, when Hazeem told me in greater detail how dangerous Vassa Praevia was—it carries a 70 per cent mortality rate for mother or baby or both—I broke down in tears. 'He's a very special baby,' my doctor said. I have no doubt that Hazeem's skill saved my life and Fenton's, and I will always be grateful to him.

But we weren't out of the woods yet. Fenton was so tiny that, despite having been given injections in the womb to help his lungs develop, he couldn't breathe unaided yet. He remained in an incubator for five weeks and Richie and I spent as much time as we could sitting beside him, willing him to grow bigger and stronger. He was a beautiful baby, with dark blue eyes and blond hair, and I melted with love for him. All I wanted was to be able to take him home. But week after week we were told we must wait.

During that time I continued to live at the hospital, spending all my time with Fenton in the premature baby unit, while Richie lived at home with Charley but came to the hospital every day. Friends and family came to see him—including Ted and Mum, in what turned out to be a brief truce in our feud—and Dad and Marcelle, but they all had to see him through a glass screen as his immune system wasn't developed and the risk of infection was too high. Only Richie and I were able to hold him. He was too small to feed, so I spent hours attached to a pump expressing breast milk for him. I felt like a prize cow and it was horribly uncomfortable, but it was worth it because I knew it would give him the best chance. He was so tiny that we used to wrap him in our T-shirts, turning the front into a pouch.

While Fenton was still in hospital, Richie and I went down to Chelsea Register Office in the King's Road to register the birth. It's a beautiful building and both of us said, 'Wouldn't this be a lovely place to get married?' We looked at each other and laughed and Richie added, 'Come on—let's book it now.' So we booked it that day, for 1 August. Fenton was due to come home a couple of weeks earlier and we thought it would be a lovely way to celebrate. It had been such a scary time that it made us want to be as solid and committed to one another as we could.

229

All we wanted was a quiet wedding. After the grief of Richie's dad dying, the falling out with Mum and the trauma of Fenton's birth we just wanted the simplest, no-fuss day possible. I couldn't have faced asking loads of people or making lots of arrangements—I just wanted to be married to Richie, without all the frills. We asked my friend Toni and her partner Kevin—who was one of Richie's best friends—to be our witnesses, and decided not to mention it to anyone else. We worried that our families would be hurt when we eventually told them, of course, but equally we knew that neither of us could cope with a big occasion. Perhaps selfishly, we decided to put our own feelings first and do it the way we wanted, even though it might leave us with some fences to mend afterwards.

At last, five weeks after his birth, the doctors decided Fenton was ready to leave hospital. We couldn't wait. Richie got everything ready at home and I was all packed and ready to go when the paediatrician called us to one side and said that unfortunately Fenton couldn't leave after all. His oxygen levels had fallen and he needed to stay under observation for another week. It was a cruel blow—we had been so sure that at last the four of us would be home together. And of course we worried about Fenton. During the next week I sat with him, telling him all about home and the life we would make for him, while he stared up at me with his amazing blue eyes.

At last, at the end of the sixth week, we were allowed to take him. Richie came to get us and I carried Fenton carefully down to the cab, where we put him into a little car seat. It felt strange to be leaving the hospital at last—I had been there for two and a half months and it had become like a second home. So many of the staff—all of them kind, hard-working and cheerful—had become friends, and I felt very tearful saying goodbye to them all. One of them, a girl called Simone, told me she was going back home to Australia soon, and I said how much I'd love to visit her country. Little did I know how soon that opportunity would come up.

I was so glad to be at home again, with a healthy baby. But, despite the fact that I was still exhausted, there wasn't much time to sit around because Richie and I had less than a week to go to our wedding day. And although it was going to be as simple an affair as possible I had to have something to wear. I was still wearing those big post-caesarean knickers, so I wasn't exactly feeling glamorous and I needed something loose and easy. I went down to the West End to look for an outfit and found a skirt and jacket that seemed right. But when I got them home and tried them on again they were too tight and didn't look right. The next day I went back to change them, and that's when I spotted a simple cotton frock in the summer sale at Brown's. It was comfortable, it fitted me and it was white, so I decided it would do.

On the day Richie set off with Kevin in one of the two cars we'd hired and I followed with Toni in the other. We girls took Kevin and Toni's three children as well as Charley and Fenton, and that was it. I wore my white dress, a Jade Jagger leather choker with sparkling strands hanging from it, a diamanté clip in my hair and pink wedge ankle-strap shoes. I felt perfect.

When we got to the Register Office Richie produced a beautiful bouquet of flowers he'd secretly ordered from a florist down the road. I hadn't thought about flowers, but he wanted me to have some. I was really touched, but the arrangement was so enormous that I was swamped by it, so he ran back and got them very quickly to make up something smaller. In the end it was perfect: pink and purple and green, which added just the right splash of colour.

Everything was so relaxed and easy. Richie hates ties so he wore an open-necked white shirt and black trousers, and Charley had a new shirt for the occasion too. He gave me away, leading me shyly into the marriage room by the hand. We hadn't thought about music, but the Registrar offered us some and I chose to go in to Minnie Riperton's 'Lovin' You'.

The ceremony was beautiful, simple and just right, and we exchanged gorgeous platinum wedding bands which Charley carried and laid carefully on a cushion when the Registrar gave him the nod. The rings had been made by a friend of Richie's in Hatton Garden, and each had the date inscribed inside it.

Afterwards we all went to one of my favourite restaurants, Zilli Fish, in Brewer Street, Soho. The owner, Aldo Zilli, a warm, generous Italian, knew us well because we'd eaten there so often. When I'd booked I didn't tell him we were getting married—I just asked him to make a nice cake for a friend's birthday, but not to write 'Happy Birthday' on it. When we arrived and he realized we'd got married he said he wished he'd known because he'd have made more fuss of us. But that was exactly why I hadn't told him—we didn't need a fuss. As it was, we had a wonderful meal: Richie and I had lobster and pasta, while Charley had fish and chips. Aldo's cake was gorgeous, full of fruit and mascarpone, and we had champagne to wash it all down.

Afterwards we went home feeling real happy about it all. But then we had to break the news to our families, because we knew it would soon come out in the press. Originally we hadn't intended to let the press know about the wedding, but *Now* magazine found out and offered us a huge sum to buy some of the pictures taken by a friend of ours. It was money we really needed and so we agreed, sincerely hoping that it wouldn't offend our families. We decided that as they were already likely to be very upset, selling the pictures probably wouldn't make things any worse.

Letting our families know wasn't easy. I told Harry and he was fine about it—he quite understood the way we'd wanted to do things. But I heard later that Mum was very upset, and Richie's family were devastated. They just couldn't believe we'd gone and done it without including them. We tried to explain that we had wanted them all there, but it just felt too complicated and too much for me after all I'd been through with the baby. Thankfully, everyone forgave us in the end.

A week or so later *Now* magazine put us on the cover and had an eight-page spread inside, and of course the rest of the press picked up on it. I found their reaction very hard to take, though I did my best to brush it off. There was a lot of criticism of my outfit and the way I looked—one critic said, 'Someone buy her a mirror for a wedding present' and another said I looked like 'a gypsy on speed'. It hurt me. This was our wedding, and if I didn't look as glamorous as they'd expected it was because I'd just been through a huge ordeal and was absolutely wiped out.

Richie had always wanted a simple little wedding, and I'd been through the extravaganza thing once already. This time it was about how much we loved one another, and making a solid future for our boys. I do sometimes think that I'd love to marry Richie again, looking more glamorous, and with all our family and friends there. Perhaps we'll get round to it one day.

After Fenton's birth I soon lost my pregnancy weight and got back in shape with the help of a personal trainer. I really enjoyed it, so when a friend suggested I make a fitness video I thought it was a great idea. I made a dance-style video with the help of a trainer whom the production company sent along, a really nice girl called Nicky. I loved doing it, and to my surprise it was a huge success. There weren't as many fitness videos around then, which undoubtedly helped, and mine went to the top of the video charts and stayed there longer than any other fitness video ever had. It was ahead of blockbusters like *Gladiator*, which I thought was hilarious. I went on to make more videos and ended up setting up my own production company—FREK Productions, named after Fenton, Richie, Emilia and Charley.

Around this time I also took on an assistant to make sure that all my fan letters and invitations were answered. Charlotte Cutler was the sister of Fran, a friend of mine, and we often bumped into one another at parties. It was Fran who had suggested Charlotte when I said I needed someone a couple of days a week. At first I wasn't sure about employing someone so close—what if it all went wrong? But I decided to go ahead and Charlotte proved wonderful, a model of efficiency and a really nice person to have around. We soon became firm friends.

Meanwhile, two weeks after our wedding I was offered a part in a film for Sky TV called *Do or Die*, about two girls backpacking around Australia and having all kinds of adventures. The other girl was to be played by a friend of mine, Kate Ashfield and the project would involve spending four months based at Bondi Beach. Although it seemed very soon to be going back to work, I loved the idea of something so different—and in Australia, too! I had signed up to do the BBC drama series *McCready and Daughter* the following year, so I had a few months to spare and this film sounded like the ideal job to fill the gap.

Richie told me to go for it—he was willing to put everything on hold to bring the kids and come with me. I'd never have gone without them, but the idea of the whole family going on an adventure together sounded great. Charlie's school agreed to let him miss a term, and friends offered to look after our house and dog. So I said yes, and a month later Richie, Charley, three-month-old Fenton and I were on a plane, flying first-class to Sydney.

15

BABY NUMBER THREE

We had a wonderful few months in Australia. I had always thought I would enjoy it there, and I did. Most amazing of all, we bumped into Simone, the nurse I'd got to know in the hospital when I was having Fenton.

I loved the Australians' attitude to life. They work to live, rather than living to work. When the director's wife had a baby during the shoot, their fourth child, a little girl with ginger hair, everything ground to a halt while he took a couple of weeks off. And every day we wrapped up filming by five and went down to the beach for a barbie, grabbing the cold beers from the fridge on the way. It was a joy to join in the relaxed and easygoing lifestyle that everyone, no matter how high-flying their job, seemed to share.

One of my co-stars was Hugo Speer, who'd been in *The Full Monty*, and we became great friends. He spent hours playing on Charley's GameBoy—the two of them became good mates and later Charley made him as a gift of the GameBoy.

It wasn't all work, though—we got the opportunity to see some of the great sights of Australia. On one occasion we went to the Great Barrier Reef and flew over to Hamilton Island. But on the way there I started to feel terribly sick. I thought it must be the motion of the small plane we were in, but I went on feeling sick all though our stay. It wasn't due to any noxious substances, as it had been so many times in the past—I wasn't totally clean during our stay, but I took very few drugs and didn't drink a great deal. After Fenton's birth I'd promised myself not to go back to my old ways and, although I smoked some puff, for the most part I managed to keep my addiction under control. It was always lurking there—I knew I still had the potential to binge and screw things up again at any time; but being in Australia, away from all the people I knew who did drugs, and therefore away from easy access to drugs, helped a lot.

When we got back to Sydney from our trip to Hamilton Island we found dozens of paparazzi cameramen outside our house. The press had tracked me down and wanted pictures. It was too much for Richie and the children and me, so the location company moved us to a gorgeous flat in Pott's Point, overlooking the Sydney Opera House. Because I was still feeling sick I decided there'd be no harm in doing a pregnancy test. I told myself I was mad—I'd only just had a baby, and besides, I was back on the Pill, so I couldn't possibly be pregnant again. But the test was positive—a shock to both of us.

In Australia they have drop-in scan centres, so Richie and I went to one of these where they told me I was four to five weeks pregnant, which meant that the baby was due in July. I had got pregnant again only four months after having Fenton. We could hardly believe the news, and of course we both became terribly anxious that the condition I'd had during my last pregnancy would recur. I'd barely had time to recover yet I might be about to go through it all again, and our new baby too might be at risk.

I was also worried about how another pregnancy would affect my contract to appear in *McCready and Daughter*. I contacted my agent, who came back to me and said that the BBC were fine, I could go ahead and they would find ways to cover up my bump once it showed. 'You can carry plants and saucepans around,' she said.

Once I knew I was pregnant again I stopped smoking puff, and once again this wasn't hard because I felt so sick. Despite this, much to our relief, doctors in Australia reassured us that I was highly unlikely to have Vassa Praevia again. This had every chance of being a normal, healthy pregnancy, they promised.

I got through the rest of the shoot in spite of my sickness, and even enjoyed it because everyone was so friendly and laid back. We had a wonderful Christmas in Fiji, and by the time we flew home Richie and I agreed that we might even contemplate emigrating.

Work on *McCready and Daughter* was due to start almost immediately. I wasn't sure how easy it was going to be as I was feeling so unwell, but I couldn't afford—in career terms or financially—to say no. At home Richie was going to be holding the fort, looking after Charley and Fenton. He said he'd bring Fenton down to the set to see me, which would be brilliant because otherwise I would miss him so much. Then, tragically, the actor lined up for the part of McCready, Tony Doyle, died suddenly of a heart attack, just as Ray McAnally had when I was due to shoot *First and Last*. On that occasion Joss Ackland had stepped in; this time it was Lorcan Cranitch, a wonderful actor best known for roles in *Cracker* and *Ballykissangel*.

I really liked Lorcan and my other co-stars, but I didn't have the happiest time shooting the series. Once again I was under Hazeem's care, which was reassuring, but I was unwell most of the time, suffering from my usual sickness plus high blood pressure and terrible migraines. At first there was no on-set nurse and it was a very male team, so there was no one who knew how I felt or who could supply a cup of tea and some sympathy. In addition to—or perhaps because of—feeling unwell I had a big argument with one of the runners on set which ended with her getting the sack. I never wanted that to happen, and felt bad about it for a long time afterwards.

As if I didn't have enough on my plate, we had to move house at this time too. In fact we had decided to do so some time earlier, but the trip to Australia had delayed it. We had chosen a place in Essex, close to Charley's school: Repton Park was a beautiful new estate with a gated entrance, big houses, garages and its own gym. It seemed amazing that we could afford to live in a place like that—I kept wanting to pinch myself. It felt like a just reward for all my hard work. We chose our house while it was still being built—it was one of the first on the estate and I just fell in love with it when I saw the plans.

We managed the move and began to settle in, but I was finding filming harder and harder going. In the end we shot only nine episodes instead of ten, because I was just too ill. The first one was shown at the beginning of June, by which time I was hugely pregnant and relieved just to have some time at home. The series was well received and a second was planned, but it was later dropped and I was never quite sure why—perhaps the ratings weren't quite as strong as expected.

Meanwhile I had to prepare for another birth, only a year after the last. Hazeem had warned me that I would need a caesarean again; towards the end of the pregnancy he became concerned about my blood pressure and decided that the baby would have to be delivered two weeks early. When I checked into the Portland Hospital TV presenter Gaby Roslin was in the next room, waiting to give birth to her son Jack. We spent hours chatting— both of us a bit nervous—as we prepared for our big moment.

The evening before my caesarean was due, the anaesthetist came to talk to me. I was sure that something was wrong as soon as I saw him. He explained that rather than having an epidural, which would anaesthetize me from the waist down, I might have to be fully unconscious. No real problem, he continued, it was just because of the way the baby was lying and the kind of caesarean they would probably need to do. I agreed, of course, but I was nervous. Was there something they weren't telling me?

The next day, 7 July, I was wheeled into the operating theatre where they decided, much to my relief, that I wouldn't need the full anaesthetic after all. I was so glad—I wanted to be conscious and to hold my baby as soon as possible. I hadn't been able to do that with Fenton as he'd been whisked off to special care, so this time I wanted everything to be right.

Richie was there, filming the whole thing, as our daughter was born. She was whisked away for a few seconds, I heard her cry, and then she was handed to me—a little moppet with a cloud of black hair. I learned later that the cord had been around her neck, which was why there had been some concern. She'd been a bit blue when she arrived, so had been taken off for a whiff of oxygen, and by the time she was given to me she was pink and perfect.

We decided to call her Emilia, after Richie's father. She had inherited his marvellous Spanish looks, with dark hair and dark eyes. Richie looked at her and said, 'Oh, my God, isn't she beautiful?' And she was. I was fascinated that none of my children had inherited my red hair—the boys are both very blond. Perhaps it will skip a generation again and, having passed from my grandfather Ginger to me, will come out in my grandchildren. Charley, who was then nine, and thirteen-month-old Fenton were brought in to meet her, and both of them were fascinated to have a sister. I found it hard to believe that I'd got a daughter, and spent hours just looking at her and thinking about all the fun we'd have together as she grew up.

That was one of the many times when I really missed Mum. I remembered her telling me how she had felt, having a daughter after two sons, and here I was, in exactly the same position, feeling it was a miracle. Yet because of my stubbornness I couldn't share it with her, or show off her first granddaughter. We hadn't spoken for over a year, since Fenton's birth. No doubt Mum missed me too, but I had been so rejecting of her that I knew she would wait for me to make the first move. And despite wishing that we'd never fallen out, I still wasn't willing to pick up the phone and say sorry.

Two days later I was allowed home after a warm goodbye to Hazeem, who once again had cared for me so well. Back at home it was chaos, with two babies to look after and the very different needs of a nine-year-old. Just trying to get them all out of the house at the same time was a major operation which could take a couple of hours. But I loved it. I had the family I'd always wanted, and that meant everything to me.

A few weeks after Emilia's birth I made another fitness video, an urban workout for busy mums, which I produced myself, through my company. We made it at the gym owned by the sister of Guy Ritchie, Madonna's husband, and Charlotte, who was still my personal assistant, did a lot of the organizing and was a fantastic help. The video did well and we talked about making a third one, in Ibiza.

A little while earlier I had learned, through press reports, that the lead part in *Red Cap* had gone to another ex-*EastEnders* actress, Tamzin Outhwaite. I had no idea why, and I was hurt that no one had contacted me personally to tell me after I'd been so involved in the development of the series. But I had long ago learned that in showbiz, as in life, nothing is certain and you just can't count on any project until the contracts are signed. I got over my disappointment and wished Tamzin luck with it.

Other work opportunities soon came along. I was asked to be a guest presenter on the children's channel SMTV, and a few months later I was invited back to *EastEnders* to make a one-off special, intended to reintroduce Ricky to the Square. Sid had left some time after me, but had decided to go back for a while. In the special Ricky went to find Bianca in Manchester and they tried to make another go of their marriage. Of course it all went wrong and ended in tears, with Bianca handing their son Liam over to Ricky—who went back to Walford to become a single dad while Bianca disappeared off into the sunset.

I loved making that film—it was great to work with Sid again and, as always, we laughed our way through it even though the storyline was as bleak as they get. I thought long and hard about the idea of going back to *EastEnders*, but in the end I decided that it just wouldn't be a good idea. It would feel like going backwards instead of forwards, and I knew there were so many other things I still wanted to try.

Since Emilia's birth I had once again gone back to drugs. I drank, too, but drugs always had the more powerful hold over me. I smoked puff regularly and, although less frequently than before, still went out from time to time and partied on a cocktail of cocaine and Ecstasy. Hardly responsible behaviour for a mother of three, and afterwards I'd always feel guilty and sorry. But not guilty or sorry enough to stop for good. I used to convince myself that I'd reached the end, go to a Twelve Step meeting and feel that by doing so I was in recovery. I still wasn't ready to understand that just turning up at a meeting, and even telling everyone there that I was an addict, wasn't enough to stop me going back out and using again. I could admit that I was addicted, but not that I needed help. I still thought I could kick drugs alone, despite the fact that after several years of attempting to do so, I had never succeeded.

Richie, patient, good-humoured and as supportive as ever, commented very little on whether I drank and used or not. If I was hungover or sick after using he would get up, sort the kids out and carry on, giving me time to recover. Luckily, as a self-employed cabbie he could choose his own working hours, which was a great help. I felt guilty, but not because he tried to make me feel bad. Far from it—Richie was wonderful to me and I was lucky to be with him. Most men would have been angry, or called me irresponsible, but Richie never did, and that made me want to clean up my act more effectively than if he'd blown up at me. I knew he was a wonderful man and I wanted to find a way to change, for him as well as for me.

At one point I decided I would only ever drink Laurent Perrier rosé champagne—which I couldn't possibly have afforded more than once in a while. This seemed like a reasonable plan, but I didn't stick to it. Sometimes I'd have a glass of champagne and then move on to a few other drinks, and that would lead to me smoking some puff because I still preferred it to alcohol. I didn't do it in front of the children, but in my heart I knew that wasn't good enough, and that I needed to stop doing it at all.

Towards the end of 2002 I was asked to appear in a play called *The Night Before Christmas* at the Riverside Studios in Hammersmith. Set to run over the Christmas period, it was a hard-hitting black comedy with a cast of only four. I played a prostitute—something I'd done a number of times since my twelve-year-old Anna Scher debut. I really enjoyed being in that play, which was clever and ultimately uplifting, and decided I'd like to do more theatre. I did—in fact over the next couple of years I appeared in five more theatrical productions, all of which I loved and all of which

244

gave me a chance to show just what I could do—including tap dancing and singing!

During the spring of 2003 I appeared in *Mum's the Word*. Something like *The Vagina Monologues* for mothers, it was a series of monologues by women concerning the unspoken, tougher aspects of being a mum. Appearing alongside me were Cathy Tyson, Carol Decker (of T'Pau fame), Jenny Eclair and Imogen Stubbs. The play ran for three months, from March to June 2003, and the five of us became very good friends.

Anxious to become a moderate drinker like other people, I got into the habit of going for a drink with the girls after the show. They all drank normally—that is, a couple of glasses of wine—and I tried to do the same. But I always wanted more. It was a struggle for me to stop at one or two, and I'd go home fighting the craving for more. Still, I hadn't had a drug blitz since before I was in *The Night Before Christmas* several months earlier, so I thought I had it all under control. That was until, towards the end of the run of *Mum's the Word*, I decided to throw a party for my thirty-first birthday.

For this, by far the biggest party I'd ever thrown, I hired a West End club and invited five hundred people. I ordered champagne and strawberries, bought myself a gorgeous outfit by Alexander McQueen, and had my hair and make-up professionally done. Richie and I booked into a hotel in St Martin's Lane for the weekend, while the children went to his mother. I wanted everything to be perfect, and by the time the party was due to start it was.

As guests began to arrive, I hit the champagne. I

told myself I deserved a glass or two. After all, I'd been 'good' for a long time, I reasoned, so why shouldn't I have a treat? One 'treat' led to another. I gulped down champagne and followed it with several tablets of Ecstasy and a gram of cocaine. Within an hour I was stumbling around and starting to black out. Despite this I took more Ecstasy—I probably had five or six pills in all—and kept going right through that night, moving on to another party after mine had ended.

By the time we got back to our hotel the next morning I had lost my bag and coat, spilt wine all down my new outfit and wrecked my new boots— and I couldn't remember anything about my party. All the pleasure I might have had in seeing family and friends and enjoying my birthday had been lost in a black fog of drugs.

Back at the hotel I became so ill that I couldn't lift my head from the pillow and thought I was going to die. It was the same way I used to feel after an all-night binge in the old days. And here I was, doing the same thing all over again. I cringed, thinking of all the people I cared about seeing me in that state. I might have got away with it when I was younger, but now I was a mother of three and it really wasn't such a good look. How was I going to face them all again?

Richie, concerned about how ill I was, picked up the pieces for me. He rang his mum and asked her to keep the children for another day. He also had to call the theatre and say I wouldn't be there for that evening's performance. I was letting everyone down, just because of my inability to control myself.

I was so ill that I felt shaky for days and, afraid

I'd done myself some permanent damage, wouldn't let Richie leave my side. I had shocked myself so much that I decided to go and see a psychotherapist recommended by Harry. He had by this time trained as a psychotherapist himself and had begged me to get help, as indeed had Richie. I had reluctantly been to see the psychotherapist once before, but I'd arrogantly told her a pack of lies and walked away, convinced I didn't need her. This time the arrogance was gone. I told her I'd lied to her before and that I needed help. She explained that I was suffering from the after-effects of a huge amount of drugs and must go home and take a few days to recover. After that I could go to see her, or join a recovery programme.

I never went back to see her. Instead I returned to the Twelve Step meetings, but it didn't help me because I wasn't really working the Twelve Steps. All I was doing was sitting there and listening to others talking about it and still believing that I didn't really need to join them.

One day I had a visit from my old friend Jo, the girl who'd stayed with me in my little Bethnal Green flat and again in my first little house after I split up with Nick. Jo had got together with snooker star Ronnie Sullivan, and by an amazing coincidence they were neighbours of ours in Essex. Jo knew I was still drinking and smoking puff and she asked me why. 'We used to laugh at you for going to fellowship meetings,' she said. 'I feel bad about that now, because you were right to go. But if you're going, how come you're still messing about? It's time you stopped using—for good.'

'Don't worry, Jo,' I told her. 'I'm fine—I can handle it. I'm not drinking or using much, just the

247

odd little bit.' I could hear myself trying to convince her, and I knew that she didn't believe a word I said. She knew that 'I can handle it' was another way of saying, 'I'm not willing to admit I've got a problem and I need help.' Jo was too nice to say, 'You're fooling yourself', but she didn't need to. I could see it in her eyes.

Swinging between being desperate for help and denying that there's a problem at all, as I was doing, is all part of the addiction pattern. I'd go to Twelve Step meetings in tears because I wanted help so badly, then when a friend like Jo confronted me I'd insist there was no problem at all. It was crazy behaviour, but I just wasn't ready to confront my addiction fully, with all the consequences.

I went on going to meetings, telling myself I was dealing with my problems when in truth I wasn't. I just couldn't bring myself to admit to a room full of strangers that I needed help, preferring to tell myself that I was doing just fine. I had a kind of restlessness that nothing seemed to satisfy. I tried getting really fit by going to the gym and swimming, but although it was nice to feel fit it didn't stop the restlessness. So I started going shopping in an attempt to make myself feel better. Soon I was shopping all the time, and spending ridiculous amounts. I had saved a lot of money, but I didn't know how long it would have to last me. I loved the theatre, but it didn't pay especially well, so I needed to be careful with finances. Richie earned money from driving his cab, but he had to take time off to look after the children whenever I was working and so he couldn't always put in long hours. Buying clothes and things for the house was bad enough. But my spending started escalating out of control when one day I set out to buy us a new car. We needed a seven-seater Jeep for all the kids, so I walked into a Mercedes showroom and bought one. It cost £38,000. I also bought a convertible sports car that cost £45,000, and that we certainly didn't need.

When I got home and told Richie what I'd done, he sat with his head in his hands. It was rare for him to get angry with me, but this had pushed him to the limit. 'Can't you see you're obsessed?' he exclaimed. 'Shopping has just taken over from drugs.'

He was right. I was, just as I always had been, trying to find a way to make myself feel better.

16

GOING INTO BUSINESS

In the spring of 2003 we had another serious problem to face. Emilia, who was almost two, had developed worrying chest problems. At a few months old she'd had pneumonia, and since then she'd had recurrent chest infections. She was the kind of baby who went quiet rather than screaming when she felt ill, so it wasn't always easy to tell, and we'd had a few scary moments when we realized she was very unwell and had to rush her to a doctor. She'd had a deep cough for some time and we'd been told first that she had asthma, although it transpired that that wasn't the explanation. The doctors couldn't work out what was wrong, so we

249

tried everything: she had allergy tests, we changed her milk and food, but nothing shifted that cough.

Then one day the mum of one of her friends at nursery asked if it could possibly be a collapsed lung. I was shocked, but this mum explained that she'd seen a case before which exactly matched Emilia's symptoms. I took her to the doctor and asked whether it might be possible, and was told no. But the suspicion wouldn't go away. I kept thinking about what the other mum had said, and the next time Emilia began coughing we took her straight to Great Ormond Street Hospital. She had a number of tests and we were warned that she might have cystic fibrosis, which was a terrifying prospect. We were still in shock when they came back to tell us that, as my friend had guessed, part of her lung had collapsed. The poor baby had brown pus in her lung, and when the doctor described it to me I was so shocked that I promised myself I'd never smoke again. I'd never smoked in front of the children, but now I felt guilty that I'd ever smoked inside the house at all, worrying that the smoke might have lingered and made Emilia's condition worse. Not to mention what it was doing to my own lungs.

Emilia was in hospital for ten days while her lung infection was treated, and the doctors explained that once it had cleared up the lung would reinflate on its own. I stayed with her through that time, while Richie took care of the boys and visited us as often as he could.

Once Emilia was well again I decided to go ahead with the plan to make a third fitness video in Ibiza. Richie and I left the children—the first time we'd been away from them—with his mum and flew out for a week to look for locations. Several other friends, including Charlotte, came with us. And of course I drank and smoked puff there, telling myself it was fine because I was on holiday and that was different from doing it at home. I was so good at kidding myself that I could have got a PhD in self-delusion. But this time I couldn't stop thinking about what I was doing, and how I'd promised myself not to do so any more. It had begun to feel as if I was doing it against my own will, and I began to realize that perhaps that was what addiction was.

While I was fighting an inner battle over my drinking and drug-taking, the seeds of another idea were being sown. One day Charlotte and I were lying on the beach and started to look at all the tanned bodies around us. Plenty of them were wearing fake tan, and it was easy to pick them out because not a single one looked really natural or even. I'd worn fake tan because with my pale, freckled skin I could never get a real one in the sun; and for the last few years I'd made sure it was high protection too. In the past I hadn't bothered with high factor protection but just lain out in the sun or on a sunbed and roasted. Then in my last year at *EastEnders* I'd had a skin cancer scare. A couple of moles had appeared on my skin, which the doctor thought could be dodgy. They had to be cut out and sent for tests to see if I had melanoma, a very fast and invasive type of skin cancer. Thank goodness I didn't, but the ten days during which I waited for the results were a frightening time, and since then I'd been much more careful.

But while I had the right protection level, the fake tan I was using looked much too orange to be

251

convincing. 'I wish I could find something that really works for skin like mine,' I moaned. As we chatted I had an idea. Why not produce and market our own fake tan, one that really would do the job? 'Do you fancy doing it with me?' I asked Charlotte. 'Definitely,' she said, 'let's go for it.' I promised myself I'd do something about it as soon as the video was finished.

Soon after that trip Richie and I went back to the island for a month, taking the children with us, to film my Ibiza workout video. Richie's mum and sister joined us for two weeks and we had such a good time that we even thought about buying an apartment out there, though in the end we decided against it.

Back home I agreed to do another play, *Squint*, which had four weeks of rehearsals followed by a four-week run at the Chelsea Theatre. I played a self-harming cocaine addict who craved love. Nothing to identify with there! I was thrilled to get some very good reviews and enjoyed the job very much.

Meanwhile Charlotte and I started to look into the idea of launching our own tanning products. I'd been going to Daniel Galvin to have my hair done for years and had become good friends with one of his sons Daniel Junior. He had launched his own organic product range, so I went and talked to him about it. 'It's not as difficult as you think,' he said. He gave me the number of a man who worked with beauty companies to launch new ranges. I called him, and we arranged a meeting at which he told us what would be involved, and gave us an introduction to a company which develops new products.

We were excited by the possibilities, and determined to get it right. We'd both have to invest money, and we wanted to be sure we were making the right investment. So we set to work to uncover a few more details. For the next few weeks we researched the cosmetics industry as thoroughly as we could. We looked into the tanning market, the kinds of ingredients used in products, the marketing side and the cost analysis.

By the end of it we could both have done a degree in the development of cosmetics. We were proud of ourselves: it was important to us to understand the process and know exactly what we were putting our names to before we got any further involved. I was actually surprised by how much I'd enjoyed learning about business. But I was totally determined to be in control of the process, having spent so much of my life feeling out of control. I didn't want other people to do this for me. After a lot of thinking and planning we decided to go ahead. We had come up with what we wanted in a fake tan: it had to be natural-looking, good for light skins, easy to apply, as far as possible without chemicals and without a strong smell.

We met the scientists at the product development company and talked it through, telling them the kinds of ingredients we wanted, and they told us what they might be able to do. We gave them the go-ahead, and when they called us to say they'd finished and had a product sample that we could go and test we were very excited. After a couple of minor adjustments we got exactly what we'd dreamed of—a light, moisturizing, natural fake tan. We were delighted with it and felt that all our hard work had paid off.

Next we set to work to design our packaging, which took several weeks, and once we'd done that Charlotte, who had had considerable experience in PR, went to see buyers at a number of major stores to find out whether they would consider stocking it. To our delight Selfridge's, one of London's oldest, classiest and most successful department stores, was very interested and indeed agreed to launch our products for us.

In the autumn of 2003 the Palmer-Cutler range of tanning products was launched at a reception in a London hotel, at which beauty writers were invited to try the products and talk to us over lunch. They were hugely enthusiastic and seemed genuinely to think that we'd come up with a great idea. After it was over I went home and thought, *I'm an entrepreneur now.* It was a good feeling, so very different from anything I'd done before, a brand new string to my bow. I just hoped that all the hard work and investment would be worth it.

It was. Our range took off beyond our wildest dreams and won the 2004 *Sunday Times Style* magazine award for Best New Beauty Product. This felt like a real achievement, because it was the readers who voted for us. The editor of the magazine commented that 'there were some very jealous beauty houses out there', which we also took as a great compliment because we'd taken a lot of our inspiration from these same beauty houses and were in awe of them.

Then GMTV did a test in which six women were each given a different tanning product to try. No one was told the name of the product they were testing until after the result—and again ours came out best. I was in hospital at the time, having my tonsils out because I was always getting tonsillitis. I tried to cheer and was in agony, but I did manage to phone Charlotte to say, 'Yippee, we did it again!' After that we were featured in a number of magazines, and soon we had a substantial following.

In six months we had recovered our initial investment and shops queued up to sell it. Soon it was in Boots, Tesco and Asda as well as many upmarket department stores. A whole range of famous people told us they used it and loved it, and we got busy developing more products for the range. We repeated our launch party after six months, and now we do it regularly twice a year. We show off our latest products—we've added lots more to the range—and offer the beauty writers, whose opinion is so important, a chance to try our products out and catch up with us.

It has felt really good to have something other than acting as a source of income. Acting will always be my first love, but I discovered that I had quite a flair for business and enjoyed it. Launching the products, and keeping our line developing and our profile high, involved going to all kinds of business meetings, taking on employees and giving presentations—and sometimes we found ourselves talking to unexpected audiences. One day Charlotte and I had to go Peterborough to talk to the cable shopping channel about selling our products. We were sitting in Starbucks at St Pancras when we looked up to see Ann Widdecombe, one of the Conservatives' front-bench MPs, standing there. A minute later the Duchess of Kent hurried past us. When we got to our train we could see several security men beside it. We thought they must be for the Duchess, until we got on the train and noticed Tony Blair sitting three seats in front of us. And it wasn't even a first-class carriage. We gawped and one of the security men came over, grinned and whispered, 'Do you want to come and say hello? Mr Blair would be happy to see you.'

Of course we did, though I wondered what on earth I'd say. When we got to Tony's seat he looked up and said, 'Patsy Palmer, how are you?' All I could say was, ' 'allo, Tone!' He invited us to sit down and have a chat, and we told him all about our cosmetics company. A couple of his women colleagues said, 'Yes, we know your products— they're great', so we were very pleased. We stayed for a while, and Tony was charming.

At the beginning of 2004 I had another first—my agent called to say I'd been asked to audition for the Andrew Lloyd Webber one-woman musical *Tell Me on a Sunday*. 'Can you handle it?' she asked. 'I'd love to give it a go,' I said. I hadn't sung since I did *Joseph* when I was six, so I really wasn't sure whether I could do it or not, but I'd always enjoyed singing. There was a week or so to go before the audition, so I went for a couple of hasty singing lessons and then, on the appointed day, headed for producer Bill Kenwright's office. On the way there I realized I hadn't eaten and was starving, so I stopped and had some fish and chips. When I arrived I said to him, 'Sorry—I think I must stink of vinegar.' He laughed, but I realized I'd made a big mistake eating a heavy meal because I didn't sing at all well. Nevertheless I got through the audition somehow, and to my amazement I was offered the part.

Bill wanted me to share a nationwide tour with two other actress-singers, Marti Webb, who had been in the first-ever *Tell Me on a Sunday*, and Faye Tozer, who had been in the hugely successful group Steps. Despite the fact that the idea still terrified me, I agreed. I threw myself into rehearsals and singing lessons, and when we opened in late February I got a fantastic response from the audience and some really good reviews. I wasn't as frightened as I'd thought I would be—the music and the wonderful songs just took over. Since the show tells a story—of a girl who goes to New York looking for love—I looked on it as an acting part in which I happened to sing, and that helped me to feel less nervous. I found singing was still as great as it had always been, and I loved being on my own on stage.

Over the next seven weeks I appeared in Sunderland, Aberdeen, Bradford, Windsor, Brighton and Wimbledon, alternating with the other two actresses who were appearing in other cities. I missed the children, but wherever I was performing Richie would bring them to see me. They loved watching me on stage—for the little ones it was the first time they'd seen Mummy act, and they found it very exciting.

After *Tell Me on a Sunday* I was seen in the BBC four-part adaptation of the period drama *He Knew He Was Right*. Wearing period costume was a hoot, and I was appearing alongside some excellent actors including Bill Nighy and Oliver Dimsdale. I'd filmed this one before the tour, and it happened to be shown the week after I finished the run. After that I felt I needed a break, so Richie and I took the children to Cyprus for a month's holiday. It was lovely, after all my months of theatre work, to spend my evenings peacefully with my family once again.

For some time Richie and I had been thinking about moving to Brighton on the Sussex coast. I had loved the place ever since Sid Owen and I spent a weekend there once, during our time on *EastEnders*. Richie was keen on it too, and we decided that if we weren't going to go and live in Australia then Brighton, with its beautiful seafront and wonderful beaches, was the next best place.

So we sold our house in Essex and found a house in Brighton—but then lost it. We decided to move there anyway and rent, so that we could be on the spot next time the right house came up. I felt so sure that Brighton was the perfect place to be. I loved the idea of being so close to the sea, and taking the kids to the beach all the time. Not long afterwards we found what we wanted—a large Victorian terrace property—but it needed complete renovation so we continued to live in our rented flat while the work was being done. The flat was quite small and it was a struggle at times, with two adults and three children and most of our stuff in storage. It was more like camping than anything else—which might have been fun for the kids, but I couldn't wait for the day we'd be once more in a proper home of our own.

In the meantime I went back to the theatre. Imogen Stubbs, one of my co-stars in *Mum's the Word* the previous year, got in touch to say she'd written a script called *We Happy Few* which had a part for me. She wanted it to be made into a film, but in the end it was put on as a play in 2004 by director Trevor Nunn, her partner. The three-hour-long piece was about a company of seven actresses touring Britain during World War II, putting on Shakespeare's plays. It was based on a true story, and appearing with me were Imogen herself, Juliet Stevenson and Kate O'Mara—a fantastic cast to work alongside. I played a lesbian and had to have a stage kiss with another woman every night—I got so used to doing so that by the end it didn't even feel strange any more.

At the same time I was asked to appear in a new six-part TV comedy series, *Monkey Trousers*, produced by Vic Reeves and Bob Mortimer, along with Steve Coogan. They all appeared in it, as did Alistair McGowan and Ronni Ancona. It was a fabulous opportunity to do comedy with the best in the business, but it meant I had to film during the day, then rush across town to appear in *We Happy Few* in the evening. But I managed it, and we filmed six episodes of *Monkey Trousers*, the zaniest, maddest comedy I'd ever encountered, and a lot of fun to do.

Under real pressure trying to fit everything in, I was smoking puff daily. I told myself it helped me cope, but of course it just made things worse. I hadn't had a serious drugs binge since my thirty-first birthday party, when I had given myself a nasty scare, but since then I'd been smoking puff in the evenings after the children had gone to bed and at the weekends when they were out. Every morning I'd get up not wanting to do it, promising myself that I wouldn't, knowing that I didn't want to smoke in the flat because of the children. And yet most days, either in the morning if I was at home or in the evening if I was working, there I was with a spliff in my hand, getting totally stoned. I felt ashamed and weak. I even avoided other parents at school—and left them thinking I was too snooty to talk to them—because I felt so bad about myself. I'd been smoking again for a few weeks before I agreed to do *Monkey Trousers*. I was desperate not to, because I wanted to be fresh and clear-headed for the next day's filming and the spliff left me feeling shaky and tired. But I didn't know how to stop.

Then one day I arrived at work and one of the girls involved in the production asked me to go for a coffee with her in the break. 'I know you,' she said. 'I saw you at a Twelve Step meeting years ago.' She told me she'd been clean for ten years and then added, 'You're not OK, are you?' I admitted that I wasn't. She said, 'Phone me when you get home tonight instead of smoking, and tomorrow we'll go to a meeting together.' I felt she was an angel who'd been sent to help me and I thought long and hard about what she said. I didn't call her—I wasn't quite ready to take that step yet—although I did manage not to smoke that night. It wasn't the last time I ever smoked. But over the next couple of weeks I finally realized, truly realized, that I was an addict and needed help. I started to see, with painful clarity, what I was doing. One day I got up promising myself I wouldn't smoke. I had an important meeting to go to at lunchtime. But I simply couldn't stop myself. I smoked, got stoned and missed my meeting. That afternoon I began to realize how I avoided all the other parents at school, hiding behind my sunglasses, because the drugs made me paranoid. I felt disgusted with myself.

Recognizing that I was an addict was a huge thing, and yet the way it happened seemed so ordinary. Everything was going so well in my life. Palmer-Cutler was taking off, I had loads of work, Richie and I were happy and the children had settled into a lovely new school—Charley in the senior school, Fenton in the first year and Emilia in the nursery. We'd found our dream house and it was just a matter of time until we moved in. So much was good in my world, and yet I was slipping back into the insanity of drug-taking. Why was I risking it all?

I looked at myself in the mirror in disgust and just knew that this was the time. I had to take action and, more than that, I had to take responsibility for what I was doing. I knew all about some kinds of responsibility—I could turn up to work, earn a living, pay my bills and look after my kids. But this was a bigger responsibility, to myself and to my family, to stop running and hiding behind drugs and alcohol. I knew that as long as I was drinking and using I could never feel good about myself, and never be truly close to the people I loved. That's because using is a way of distancing yourself, not just from painful feelings but from other people.

The next day I went to a Twelve Step Fellowship convention. This was not just an ordinary meeting but a much bigger gathering. I was horribly nervous. I'd spoken in meetings before, and admitted I was an addict, but on those occasions I had just been going through the motions. Now I really knew what it meant to be an addict and that I needed to make recovery central to my life, every day of my life. So this time I spoke from the heart.

I told this huge meeting that I was an addict and had just realized it. And most important of all, I told them I needed help. I felt frightened, vulnerable and very small as I made that admission. But once I'd done it I felt my terror evaporate. A number of people came over, hugged me and said, 'Well done!', and I felt very tearful and very happy. When I got home I described the day's life-changing events to Richie, who, despite having witnessed the effects of my drug-taking and drinking, hadn't thought of me as an addict any more than I'd thought of myself as one. As always, he was supportive and proud of me.

We finished filming *Monkey Trousers* a couple of weeks later, and in November *We Happy Few* came to an end. After the run Trevor Nunn sent me a card with a photo of the cast, on which he wrote, 'Dear Patsy, You are a rare spirit. You have extraordinary innocence, natural wit, great quickness of perception, amazing humility for one so famous and an unmistakable emotional truthfulness. I have loved doing this show with you and am so thrilled you agreed to be with us on this unusual journey. Love, Trevor.' I was touched and honoured by such generous comments from someone so respected in the acting world. It warmed my heart to think that he thought so well of me. Now I just needed to find a way to feel good about myself.

17

FINDING JULIE

Soon after *We Happy Few* finished I was offered the lead role in the tap dancing comedy *Stepping Out*. It was another Bill Kenwright production, and I was flattered to be asked, but at first I said no without even looking at the script. I had done such a lot of theatre and I felt I wanted to be at home for a while. Then a friend I hadn't spoken to for ages rang me. I told her I'd just turned down a show because I wanted some time with the family. 'What was it?' she asked. When I told her it was *Stepping Out* she shrieked, 'That's a wonderful show—it's so funny you *must* do it!'

So, I went and got the script and sat down to read it, and when I saw just how good it was I knew she was right. I called Bill and told him I'd changed my mind. It was many years since I'd last tap-danced, and we only had two weeks of rehearsals, so I had to work very hard. The show—which had been made into a film starring Lisa Minnelli—was about a tap class in north London, run by a woman called Mavis Turner. An assortment of people turn up to the class—nine women and one shy man, none of them very good at tap dancing, and all of them wanting a little escapism from the rest of their lives. At first they're pretty hopeless, but they get better and better until they're fantastic. Along the way they laugh, cry and support one another.

We opened in late January 2005, toured the country until late May, and had a ball. I loved the show because it had such a feel-good factor. And I was incredibly proud of myself for getting the whole way through it without any drink or drugs. When the others went for an after-show drink I learned to say no and go for something soft, and when I got home I had a cup of tea instead of a spliff.

Ever since the Twelve Step convention the previous September I had been going to meetings regularly, several times a week, and for the first time ever I had been working the Twelve Steps. It was tough. I had to put my pride to one side and let others see my vulnerability: I had to ask for help. At every meeting I looked around and saw people who had been working the Steps for years. I'd felt different from such people, or even superior to them, in the days when I was still convinced that they were addicts and I wasn't. Now I realized that they were further down the road I was just starting on, and they knew far more than I did. They knew how hard it can be, struggling against the craving for drink or drugs, how important it is to reach out to someone else for support when you're struggling, and that you can never be complacent or say, 'I've done it.'

So now, instead of distancing myself from other addicts, I began to make connections with them, making friends, phoning—and being phoned—for support, congratulating one another on each small achievement and laughing about the many ways we'd fooled ourselves in the past. It felt good. It was hard to stick with it—there were moments when I really craved drugs. But I reasoned that I'd come to Brighton for a better life, so it didn't make sense to ruin it, and instead of reaching for a spliff

I reached for the phone and called someone to talk me through the craving until it was over. At last I understood the concept of one day at a time, and realized that I needed a support network of like-minded people to turn to.

I had fantastic support at home, too. Richie hadn't found it easy at first, when I began going to meetings almost daily and making so many new friends. Pleased as he was that I wasn't drinking or using, he was also a little afraid that I would change totally, or wouldn't need him any more. But we talked a lot and he realized that, far from not needing him, I needed him more than ever if I was going to stay clean. Richie has always enjoyed a social drink but, in a touchingly generous gesture, to support me he gave up drinking.

I haven't touched drink or drugs since September 2004. I'm pleased, but I'm not complacent. I go to meetings as often as I can and I've developed a spiritual life, which I never had before and which means a lot to me. These days, I'm happy to say that I believe in God.

As I gradually worked my way through the Twelve Steps I realised that I needed to say sorry to all the people I'd hurt or wronged over the years. That was a tough one. Could I really put my pride to one side, admit I'd been in the wrong and apologize? Could I sincerely let go of resentment and blame? To do so, I had to see that addiction and resentment go hand in hand, and to recognize how often I'd been controlling, manipulative and convinced that I was right and others were wrong. It was a revelation to admit that on many occasions I'd been the one who was wrong.

The first person I contacted was my mum. I was

scared, at first, to swallow my pride and go and see her after three years of silence. I was shaking with nerves on the train up to London. At the station I called her and asked if I could come over—and was so relieved when she said yes. If I thought there would be recriminations or rejection, I couldn't have been more wrong. Mum greeted me with open arms, and we both wept as we hugged one another. For the next few hours we talked, cried and laughed, forgave one another and became very close again. I apologized for all the hurt I'd caused her, and talked honestly about how big a part drugs had played in my life. Mum told me how hard it had been for her, suspecting that I was taking drugs but feeling unable to help and hoping against hope that I would come through it. I was able to listen to her properly, and to tell her how sorry I was to have put her through such torment.

Now we see one another often again, and Mum is a vital and much-loved part of our family. Our relationship has shifted—we aren't so much mother and child any more but two adults, and that feels good. Mum and Ted are still happily unmarried together, and Ted, as always, is a rock to everyone.

I also wanted to make amends to Nick, my first husband. During our brief marriage I'd behaved badly to him. We talked, and were able to part as good friends.

Having made such positive progress in my personal life, I was intrigued when in the summer of 2005 a different sort of challenge came along. If I'd thought tap dancing on stage every night for three months was hard, it was nothing to what I had to go through for *Strictly Come Dancing*. When

I was first approached about doing the show I laughed and said no. First of all I couldn't see myself doing all that dancing, and secondly I never agree to participate in reality TV shows. I've been asked to do just about all of them, from *Big Brother* to *I'm a Celebrity*, but I've never been interested. I thought Sid was brilliant on *I'm a Celebrity*—he was so brave, and his humour and sweetness shone through. But it wasn't for me, and neither was *Big Brother*. I've never liked the idea of being filmed sleeping, for a start.

It was Richie's mum who talked me into doing *Strictly*. When I told her I'd been asked, she jumped up and down and told me that it was one of the best programmes on TV and that I'd be great in it. And she was right to have pushed me. When I watched some past episodes I realized it's a wonderful show, with style and glamour—reality TV at its best. And once I knew that each series raises around 11 2 million for the BBC charity Children in Need it wasn't hard to allow myself to be persuaded.

I was teamed up with the lovely Anton du Beke, who must have been born dancing. We bonded immediately, and I was buoyed up by his excitement because he felt we had a fighting chance of winning. The training takes place during each week, before the Saturday night live show. In my case I could only do it four days a week between school drop-off and pick-up, which didn't give us long.

Watching the previous two series had frightened the life out of me. The winners, newsreader Natasha Kaplinsky and ex-*EastEnders* actress Jill Halfpenny, were stunningly good and I wasn't sure

I could ever approach their standard. The first day was fine and I thought, *This isn't too bad.* But we hadn't even scratched the surface—all Anton did that day was to run me through some basic steps. By the second day the honeymoon was over, and during the next couple of weeks, leading up to the first show, he really made me work.

Halfway through that first week I started to get really scared. For a start my posture was a nightmare, so I had to try to adjust that at the same time that I was trying to learn all the moves. Professional dancers make it all look so easy, but it's actually very tough. I began to think I just couldn't do it—I was stiff as a board, and on top of everything else all the twirling around made me feel incredibly sick, so I had to keep stopping. By the time we'd got through those first two weeks I was aching from head to toe.

But I was loving it too. I felt fit and graceful, and Anton was a dream to work with—kind, funny and tough enough to get the very best out of me. He's like an old-fashioned film star, born in the wrong era. When I was dancing with him I'd sometimes get tingles up my spine, because it reminded me of being a little girl in Farvy's flat, watching old black-and-white films or singing along to the wireless.

When we got to the first live performance—and, indeed, not just the first—I was incredibly nervous. I thought I wouldn't be, after all the theatre I'd been in over the previous few years. My nerves aren't usually too bad, but as we waited in the wings for Bruce Forsyth to announce us I was worse than I've ever been. The thought of dancing live in front of ten million viewers was so daunting that my heart felt as though it was about to explode out through my neck. Some of the others had a drink to calm their nerves, but, tempted as I was, I didn't join them. Instead I had a cigarette. I'd given up those too, but I decided this was an exception I'd have to make.

My first dance was the waltz. I loved the glamorous outfit and felt so feminine, swirling around the dance floor. And of course I've always responded to music—our waltz music was beautiful, and I felt it inside me like a heartbeat. But even so I really struggled with that waltz—it was so difficult trying to remember the steps and the posture while keeping a smile plastered on my face.

Anton had come third in the first series, partnering classical singer Lesley Garrett, but hadn't done so well in the second series with Esther Rantzen. He kept telling me, 'You need to get competitive.' That's never really been my style, so I laughed at him, but by the time we were ready for our first performance I really did want to do well. Nevertheless I was afraid I'd fail straightaway, because unlike many actresses I'd never been formally trained in dance. However one of the judges, Bruno Tonioli, boosted my confidence enormously when he said he'd seen me in the past, swinging myself around the dance floor in a couple of nightclubs, and he really thought I could do well. It was so encouraging of him, but I still felt that this was a completely new departure for me and I wasn't at all confident I could master it. When Mum said to me afterwards, 'Try to relax—you're so tense', it was an understatement.

It never got easier. Every week it was a struggle to learn new steps, and I found doing so even more difficult when we were being filmed during rehearsals; but I put my heart and soul into it. I knew the judges would sometimes make adverse comments and I didn't think I'd mind. After all, it's an entertainment show and the judges' no-holds-barred opinions are part of the fun. I've been a professional for so long I thought I could take anything, so I was genuinely surprised at how hurt I felt when they went through all the things I'd done wrong. Far from feeling determined to improve, I felt worse. Perhaps it was because I'd tried so hard in the first place.

My high point was the week we danced the tango, when Anton and I won top points. I was ecstatic. I'd loved learning the tango, and somehow I'd found the steps easier and my feet didn't feel so tangled up as in the other dances. I never made it to the top again, but I never gave it less than my all, encouraged by the money we were raising. I was very happy when we made it through to the last five of the original twelve couples and, although we got knocked out that week, I felt I'd done well to get that far. In fact I felt quite relieved that I didn't have to face those dreadful Saturday night nerves any more. The only woman to beat me was Zoe Ball, who came third; the other three top places went to men, and I was delighted when England cricketer Darren Gough and his professional partner Lilia Kopylova won the competition.

On the domestic front, in 2006 we finally moved into our new home after waiting eighteen months for the renovation work to be completed. Its large, airy rooms were just what we wanted: there was an attic room for Charley, so that he could have his own space, and Fenton and Emilia each had a bedroom next to ours. In the basement was a large area that we planned to turn into a family games room, with an office next to it.

With the basic furniture in place, the rest of our possessions were brought out of storage and put into this basement area so that we could unpack them bit by bit. There was no rush—we just wanted to settle in first. Then disaster struck. A few weeks later I was in London for a Palmer-Cutler meeting when a friend who was in our house phoned to say that water was pouring through the kitchen ceiling. It was so bad that I could even hear it over the phone. Trying not to panic, I called our builder. He hurried round and discovered that a pipe had burst, sending water down through the kitchen and into the basement. By the time the water was turned off and the leak fixed the basement was several inches deep in water and all our stored belongings were soaked.

Richie rushed home as soon as he heard the bad news, and by the time I got back from London things were calmer and the flood was being dealt with. But many of our possessions were ruined, and several floors and ceilings had been damaged. The thought of having to have them all redone, when they had only just been finished, was awful. But to my surprise I managed to stay quite calm. It was a turning point. A few years before I would have headed straight for oblivion with a cocktail of drugs. So I was proud of myself for accepting that I couldn't do a thing to change it, having a cup of tea and even managing to laugh about it with Richie.

That wasn't the only mishap we had around that time. A couple of weeks later we were invited to a Rolling Stones concert at Twickenham Stadium

271

and to a party at Ronnie Wood's house afterwards. I was tired that night and a couple of days later I was due to start filming a new BBC costume drama. Still, I knew the concert would be brilliant and we agreed we wouldn't come home too late, so we organized a babysitter and set off.

The evening didn't bode well when we got to the stadium box office and there were no tickets waiting for us. Thankfully Charlotte turned up at that moment, with a couple of spares she'd been given by a friend who couldn't go. But they weren't in the VIP area close to the stage—we were miles up, and Mick Jagger looked the size of a pin. I texted Sid Owen, who was due to be there too. He was in the VIP area. *Right*, I thought, *I'm not sitting up here while Sid enjoys the best view*. So we traipsed down the thousands of stairs and managed to slip in to join him.

The atmosphere was electric and Mick gave it his all, leaping about on stage in his drainpipe trousers and looking pretty sexy for a guy his age. When he sang 'Sympathy for the Devil', my favourite Stones song, it took me right back to my teens when I danced to it every Thursday night at a club in Charing Cross. This time I felt on a high without the aid of several Ecstasy tablets and a few grams of coke, and it was a good feeling.

The concert ended early because Mick's voice gave out—it turned out that he wasn't well, and he'd made a real effort to go on stage and last as long as he did. We all went back to the party at Ronnie's house, which was spectacular. I was particularly impressed with the wheatgrass bar, where every kind of smoothie you could imagine was being concocted from natural ingredients. Just what I needed—and I wasn't tempted at all by the huge range of alcoholic drinks on offer.

There was some great music playing and Charlotte and I decided to dance. We love dancing at parties, and when you're sober and most other people aren't it's often the best thing to do. So we headed for the dance floor, where the centrepiece was a tall blonde high-kicking and swinging herself around a pole stuck in the middle of the floor, much to the delight of most of the men there. At 12.30 Richie made signs for us to go, because we had a long drive back to Brighton and an early start the next day. I was heading for the loo, winding my way through the dancers, when suddenly what felt like a brick hit me in the face.

I was so stunned I didn't know at first what had happened. It was only later that I realized the pole dancer had inadvertently kicked me as I walked past. With a tooth sticking through my bottom lip and blood everywhere, the pain was excruciating and I thought I was going to black out. Terrified that all my teeth had been smashed I staggered onwards to the loo, my hand over my mouth. Luckily Jo Wood, Ronnie's wife, saw me and came to help. I was in shock and I began to cry, my whole body shuddering with sobs. Jo got her housekeeper to take me into the kitchen and give me some ice, but I was in such pain I couldn't use it. And all I could think was, *I'll lose my BBC job—they won't be able to film me like this.*

Someone got Richie and he put me in the car and drove me to the nearest hospital, where thank goodness there was no queue in the accident and emergency department.

'How did you do this?' the charge nurse asked

me.

'Er, I was kicked in the face by a pole dancer.' I knew it sounded mad. Especially as I was totally sober. I don't know how the nurse kept a straight face.

My lip was stitched up, I was given antibiotics and painkillers, and Richie took me home. We arrived at three in the morning, at which point Fenton and Emilia woke up and started to cry when they saw my battered and swollen face. Richie calmed them down while I fell into bed. But I couldn't sleep—despite the painkillers my face was throbbing.

Grateful that it hadn't been worse, I soon recovered with only a small scar—though not in time for the BBC job, which I lost. But I've learned to take things in my stride now. My peace of mind becomes stronger every day and I no longer respond to crises like this one and the flood in the house by reaching for a drink or a spliff. It isn't that I'm not tempted—I am. But now I know I can deal with temptation, I can choose not to give in. Sometimes it feels as though I spent twenty-four years, from the age of eight to thirty-two, asleep and just pretending to be awake, getting through life in a haze of drink, drugs and adrenalin-fuelled dramas. It's a relief to wake up for real and discover that not only can I manage life without drugs, I love it.

And since I've been drug-free I've discovered a new passion—painting. I've always loved art—when I left school I'd wanted to go to art college, but I hadn't passed enough GCSEs to get in. Then in Brighton I met Julie-Anne Gilbert, a well-known local artist who had her own gallery and offered me some space in her studio to paint.

I knew I wanted to paint angels. I love them, and when we find white feathers I tell the kids that means an angel is about and their little faces light up. But when I began I wasn't at all sure what would emerge on the canvas. Whenever I had a spare moment I kept going back to the studio to add a little more, and the painting evolved until it was an angel that I felt was very special. It was vibrantly colourful, and I gave it a halo of a real pink neon light so that I could plug it in and enjoy looking at it lit up.

Painting became a kind of therapy, a valuable part of my recovery, and in the autumn of 2006 I was offered my first exhibition in Brighton. I wasn't sure what people would think of my work but it didn't matter—I had loved making the painting; and that was the main point. When the show opened I was so excited by the response. A lot of people told me they loved my paintings and asked whether I would make prints of my original angel— which I had decided not to sell. If anyone had told me five years earlier that I would learn ballroom dancing and perform live in front of millions, be a director of an award-winning cosmetics company, have my own art exhibition and write a book I would have laughed. And if they'd told me that I'd manage all that without alcohol or drugs I'd have been even more disbelieving. So it feels good—very good—to have done all these things and to have plans for so many more.

I'm proud of being a wife, mum, actress, entrepreneur, painter and writer. And right up there with the best of what I've done, I'm proud of staying clean and sober for more than two years—

so far. I believe things happen when we're ready for them. I'm getting to know myself, not the actress Patsy Palmer but the real Julie Harris, every last hidden corner of me, in a way I never could have in the past. I feel I've been given a new life, a second chance, and I'm so grateful. For the first time I know that life is about everything around me, rather than everything revolving around me.

I feel blessed, and I hope very much that through my story I can help support others who are coping with addiction. In my time I was like so many young girls who binge drink and use drugs, convinced they haven't really got a problem. I hope that perhaps a few of them will recognize themselves in these pages and ask for help, without leaving it as long as I did. Most important of all, I hope I've been able to show my three beautiful children that, with determination, honesty and the support of others, there is almost nothing you cannot overcome.